Thank you for your
friendship over the years.
Lovingly -
Helen

Wrapped in Love

The Shepherd's Protection of His Lamb...

from China to Canada

Helen Dancy Carey

Library and Archives Canada Cataloguing in Publication

CIP data on file with the National Library and Archives

ISBN 978-1-55483-845-5

Dedicated

To

Brian and Lorraine

my dear children

whose

love, loyalty, and understanding

throughout the years

have been a precious blessing

Acknowledgements

More than fifteen years ago I put pen to paper and began writing my life story by hand. Thankfully, our dear friends, George and Eleanor McCullagh, insisted that I purchase a computer for such a mammoth undertaking. With their time and patience, I was introduced into a new world of technology which has resulted in the completion of this book.

The resources I had in hand were plentiful, almost overwhelming. I owe deep thanks to John and Joanne Brock, my first cousins, and especially to their son David Brock who researched the *China's Millions* magazine in partnership with the Overseas Missionary Fellowship. I was amazed to learn of the almost unbelievable experiences of both sets of my grandparents and my parents from the Windsor and Brock generations. Thank you to the OMF Staff who so kindly high-lighted these family names. Equally, deep thanks to the late Joan Brock from New Zealand, who enlightened me with many resources of the Brock families in China. Only recently did I discover another Brock member, third cousin Jared, who in his book, *Living Prayerfully,* gave further insights about my grandfather, John Brock, in China. You have brought a "freshness" to the family archives.

With a humble and grateful heart I wish to thank the Overseas Missionary Fellowship, previously named the China Inland Mission, for their care and protection of the Windsor family throughout many decades. Your permission to quote from several OMF books is greatly appreciated.

What a wealth of information lies within the pages of the *Chefoo Magazine* which I have read for many years. A sincere thank you to the editor, Ian Grant, for your excellent work and for allowing me to include a few brief phrases here and there, related to my years spent in Kiating and Kuling. I am truly indebted to you for setting me straight on issues that required documentation. For your time and support, I am most grateful.

It was over a cup of tea with Maybeth (Tyler) Henderson that she read the important role her parents had in my life. A big thank you for allowing me to relive, more accurately, the special memories from your mother's excellent stories. Your continual encouragement to me, along with your willingness to help with the final stages of the manuscript, has meant ever so much to me.

I wish to recognize my precious friend, Margaret Pearce, who kindly let me verify facts from her story about our days in China. Your loyal friendship to me is beyond measure.

A huge thanks goes to my good friend Ann, who faithfully passes on to me the devotionals, *Every Day with Jesus*. How I treasure them. I have used several quotes in the book.

I can't say thank you enough to my editor, Jeannie (Lockerbie) Stephenson, who for so many years has been pursuing me from the beginning to the end of this production. You were needed, Jeannie, to keep me on track and focused thoughout the years, and especially during the recent months when I decided to "hit the deck," as you said. You were the right fit for me in many ways, particularly with the common bond of overseas missions, nursing affiliations, sharing cups of tea together, and the love of books. I appreciate your patience and ability to help me find a purpose later in life which I hope will enrich others.

God has given me wonderful friends who have encouraged me along the way. My special thanks goes to those who prayed for me during my many hours of writing. I am so grateful for the support of my family, including my late husband Walter, who had to put up with hearing about my story for so long. It is now done!

My deepest thanks goes to my husband, Bill, who has been extremely supportive since he took me as his bride nearly four years ago. Little did he know then, what he was in for. How good God was to give me a husband who has expertise in English grammar (a former school principal). Bill read, adjusted sentences, proof-read, encouraged me, went the extra-mile by taking on meal preparation and prayed daily for me. Thank you, Dear, for helping me to fulfill my dream.

Helen (Dancy) Carey
October 2016

CHINA INLAND MISSION

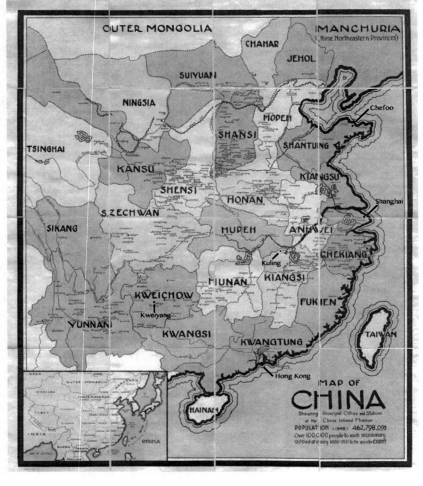

OUTER MONGOLIA

CHAHAR

MANCHURIA
(Nine Northeastern Provinces)

JEHOL

SUIYUAN

NINGSIA

HOPEH

Chefoo

SHANSI

SHANTUNG

TSINGHAI

KANSU

KIANGSU

SHENSI

HONAN

Shanghai

S.ZECHWAN

HUPEH

ANHWEI

SIKANG

CHEKIANG

Kuling

HUNAN

KIANGSI

KWEICHOW

Kweiyang

FUKIEN

YUNNAN

KWANGSI

KWANGTUNG

TAIWAN

Hong Kong

HAINAN

MAP OF

CHINA

Showing Principal Cities and Stations
of the China Inland Mission

POPULATION (1948) 462,798,093
Over 100,000 people to each missionary
999 out of every 1000 still to be won to CHRIST

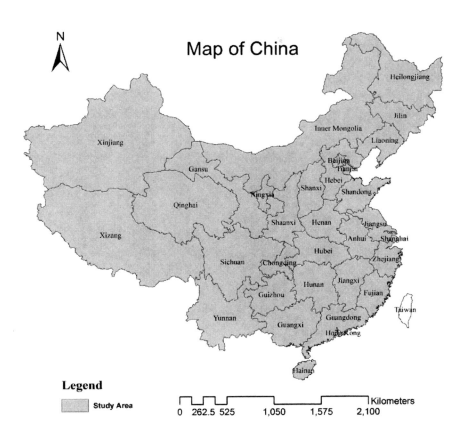

Contents

Foreword

In April 1997, I met Walter and Helen Dancy. They invited my husband, Wally Stephenson, and me to their home for a meal during a Missions' Conference at West Park Baptist Church in London, Ontario. Wally and his first wife, Louise, had been church planters in South Africa. Back in Ontario, Louise and their daughter Ruth, were tragically killed in a car accident.

After serving in Bangladesh for 33 years, I moved to the United States and opened a publishing department for our mission: Across Borders For World Evangelism, (ABWE). One manuscript I received was from Wally. Of course, we worked together on his book, *Through Tears to Triumph*. We were married in 1996 and now were representing our mission at West Park's Conference.

So there we were in the Dancy's home enjoying Sunday dinner together. In later years I saw Walter and Helen at their post at the main entrance of West Park. Those of us who were privileged to know him, still speak of Walter's smile, gracious manner and willingness to help people find a classroom, a lost coat, or whatever they needed.

When I first heard part of Helen's early history I said, "This story has to be written." From time to time I asked her—okay, I "bugged her"—about the book. She showed me books, pictures, articles, and mementoes from her China days. She invested in a computer and learned how to use it. Over cups of tea, I urged her on, until I realized she would do it in her own, and in the Lord's, timing. Through the years of Helen's loving care for Walter during his illness, grieving his death, and her adjustment to being a widow, the book was put on the back burner. And then Bill came along.

Following the deaths of their spouses, Bill and Helen were married in December 2012.

I knew Bill Carey as my brother, Bruce Lockerbie's good friend during their high school days in London. Bill's sister, Carol, married Gerald Brock who was Wally's classmate at The London Bible Institute, later named London College of Bible and Missions.

When Bill and Helen returned from Florida in April 2016, Helen, with Bill's encouragement, had already laid out the initial draft in her well-organized fashion. She was ready to "hit the deck." It has been my delight to work with her in the editing process. Again, with cups of tea to spur us on, we have spent months organizing, writing, re-writing, and telling of God's gracious guidance, as the Good Shepherd led His lamb, Helen Jean Windsor Dancy Carey.

Jeannie Lockerbie Stephenson

Preface

"The faintest ink can sometimes be better than
the strongest memory."[1]

I have always been drawn to reading biographies and autobiographies. I follow with interest the events and happenings in people's lives. Please allow me to share some of the events of my life with you. This idea has been simmering on the back burner for many years, but now in approaching my eightieth year, I have no choice but to bring it to completion.

"Every incident in all of our lives can be used by God for His ultimate purpose. Our lives are "not a series of haphazard events, but a narrative."[2]

I trust that you will be impressed with the way my God has taken all the events of my life and fit them into a pattern for good.

My original plan was to share my story just with my children, Brian and Lorraine, but many people have strongly encouraged me to make it available beyond my family. I know many others have written so well of their experiences in China. My story may pale in the light of theirs. However, the following words by Phillips Brooks as quoted in *Springs in the Valley* encouraged me:

"Find your purpose and fling your life out into it; and the loftier your purpose is, the more sure you will be to make the world richer with every enrichment of yourself."[3]

My prayer is that you will get a glimpse of how wonderfully God has cared for me, His little lamb, a missionary kid; commonly known as an MK. May the examples of His care throughout these pages be an encouragement to you. I hope you will have as much fun on this journey with me as I have had in writing it.

been. Perhaps she realized then why Dad gave her the money. She needed it to pay the Chinese men to get us to the next village, where we could stay that night in an inn.

At times these roadside inns were wretched places, where sweaty, drunken travellers, mostly men stayed. Some inns were even opium dens. Often, though, the innkeeper—or usually his wife—would sweep out a storage room or a place where a family with children could stay. I think the innkeeper (and his wife) get blamed wrongly in the Christmas story. We have been led to believe that they didn't have or didn't make room for Jesus inside the inn. In reality, they could have noticed Mary's condition and, in sympathy and compassion, moved her to a place where she could deliver the baby away from the noise and dirt of the inn. Maybe it was a storeroom. Mostly likely it was a cave in the hillside.

And so it was with us. The bodies of the two men were placed in a separate room. I still have memories of our room that night.

The next day mother and I, along with my dad's body, were taken to the to the nearest mission station. That was Pichieh, where German missionaries named Friedenshort lived. They were kindness itself, providing a suitable coffin for my dad. Mr. Michell and Mr. Ament, both of whom worked closely with my parents, arrived from Kweiyang. They brought Mother, Dad's body, and me, to the home of Bill and Muriel Rae in Anshun. These dear friends lovingly cared for us. They assured Mother that God makes no mistakes and that the Lord would never leave us. Bill also gave us a precious promise: to pray for my mother and her family daily until his death!

Later Muriel Rae told us that I said, "We were in a car and when we went around the corner, the car bumped. My daddy got off, and got on again at Heaven."

Many years later while visiting Muriel Rae in Toronto, she told me that Bill had faithfully kept his promise. How fortunate for us to be the subject of such a prayer warrior for over 30 years! I am still amazed by this, 75 years later! What a beautiful hedge of protection the Good Shepherd put around us.

The funeral took place on Sunday, October 5, 1941 at Anshun, Kweichow. I have a vague recollection of being there with Mother. A precious letter written by Muriel Rae states that "the service was beautifully solemn. The Chinese were deeply moved and so were the foreigners." A Chinese personal friend of Dad spoke for ten minutes. Many of the missionary men also gave tributes to him. Muriel writes further that "Mrs. Windsor is a very noble and brave little woman. Her faith has been tried with fire, but even now it is being found unto praise and honour and glory."

Dad was laid to rest beside his father who had died from dysentery on August 16th, 1915 at age 53.

On October 19, 1941 Emmanuel Baptist Church in Toronto held a Memorial Service. It was evident that people in his home church loved him, as indicated by the following quotes from the church bulletin:

- He made a definite and lasting contribution to the Young People's work.
- With his quiet and kindly manner, yet with a firm and steadfast devotion to the Lord Jesus, his influence was a blessing to everyone who had the great privilege of knowing and being associated with him.
- With an entire lack of ostentation, he proved himself dependable in everything to which he set his hand, particularly so in those things of apparently lesser importance.

Bishop Frank Houghton, General Director of the China Inland Mission (CIM), said of my dad; "Here was a man who had 20 years of service in China behind him, but we all believed that his best and most fruitful years lay ahead, and it is no secret that he was marked out for one of the higher administrative positions in the Mission. I was deeply impressed with his tact, patience, self-effacement, sound judgement, acceptance with his brethren, and his loyal-singleness of heart."[1]

Of course, Mother, my sister Marjory, and I were not at the Toronto service, but the words that were said were most comforting.

While on earth we may never know why a man of this calibre was taken so soon. When we get to Heaven we will know the answer, or it won't even matter. To meet my dad will be beyond description!

Chapter 2

Beginnings

"You have given me the heritage of those
who fear Your name."
Psalm 61:5

Some people have asked me, "How is it that your life began in southwest China?" I was not privileged to know my grandparents, but fortunately, I learned about both sets of grandparents by reading *China's Millions,* the publication of the China Inland Mission. It was thrilling to learn of their missionary endeavours and diligent service for the Lord during the late 1800's after they joined the China Inland Mission, founded by James Hudson Taylor in 1865.

Their early years in China were full of political unrest and turbulence, including the cruel Boxer Rebellion, a time when hundreds of people, including missionaries, were killed. In my reading, I discovered that my grandparents endured near death experiences and harassment by enemy soldiers.

The Brocks
My maternal grandparents, John and Edith (Elliot) Brock arrived in China from Scotland and England respectively.

"John Brock, as a young Scottish legal clerk, heard God's call to be a missionary to China after attending the well-known Keswick Convention in London, England in 1887, where Hudson

Taylor was speaking. John was accepted by the CIM on his 21st birthday. During his missionary service he acquired land, built a church, established the first Bible seminary in Anwhei province and was the longest-serving missionary in the region, 50 years altogether, just one year shy of Hudson Taylor's record."[1]

My mother, Edith Constance Brock, known as Connie, was born on March 1,1900 in Anking, Anwhei province. She was the second oldest and the only girl of seven children, two of whom died in infancy.

My mother attended the school for missionaries' children in Chefoo, a seaside town on the north east coast of China. This city is now called Yantai. Even though the parents found it hard to leave their children at the school, it was important for them to have a good education, allowing them to be prepared for higher education in their homelands later. The children, having many playmates, learned to get along well with their peers. There were other advantages such as Boy Scouts, Girl Guides, music lessons, and well organized sport days. Most of the children who attended the Chefoo schools came away enriched. Chefoo also enabled the parents to pursue their missionary calling whether it be teaching, preaching, medical work, or administrative duties in the various mission stations.

Because of the distance from school to home and the lengthy travel time, parents and children did not see each other for months or even years at a time. Mother remembered how hard it was to leave her parents when she was only six. A few times her parents would visit Chefoo to see their children. That also included a holiday by the sea. I know Mother went home to Anking a few times during school breaks.

Upon finishing school at age 17, Mother spent six months in Shanghai babysitting the two-year-old son of American missionaries. The money from this helped to outfit her for Canada. She also spent some months with her parents, who had moved to another province, before she sailed from Shanghai to Canada. She chose Canada because two aunts on her mother's side lived in Ontario. Later, her three younger brothers, Jack, Alan, and Gordon, after leaving Chefoo, also moved to Ontario. Her older brother, Douglas, had already gone to England.

Mother took a secretarial course that enabled her to work in an office. She had a room in a boarding house in Toronto where she was shocked to find bed bugs and cockroaches! She thought these critters lived only in China!

In 1919, a year after her arrival in Canada, she received news that her mother had died from influenza. How thankful she was to have spent those precious months with her parents prior to leaving China.

Two years later, her father married Maude Gordon, a missionary from New Zealand. They had two children, Lawrence and Joan. So my mother had a step-mother, a half brother, and a half sister. They met from time to time. For several years I have been in touch with Joan, my half-aunt in New Zealand, whom I met once when she visited Canada. We developed a warm relationship through e-mails and phone calls. In fact, Joan has given me much insight into the Brock family history. Her brother, Lawrence, became a doctor, moved to England, and raised a family there.

In the winter of 2016, I learned that my mother's older brother, Douglas, was honoured by the British Government. They featured his photograph, along with the Union Jack, painted on the East Coast Train (#91111). The mural, called *For The Fallen,* was part of the effort to commemorate the centenary of the start of WWI. The train travelled from King's Cross Station in London, England, to Edinburgh, Scotland. It was specially decorated to honour five regiments.

Upon leaving Chefoo school, Douglas went to England and worked in the Bank of Montreal in London. The Canadian soldiers cashed their paycheques at that specific branch. So most likely Douglas met John McCrae, the Guelph-born author of the iconic poem, *"In Flanders Field."*

At age 18, Douglas enlisted in the Royal Field Artillery. Douglas and John were stationed at Flanders Field. Sadly, Douglas was killed in action at age 19. He was buried with honours in the British cemetery in the village of Cheque, France.

The Windsors

My paternal grandparents, Thomas and Annie (Hastings) Windsor arrived in China from England and Canada respectively. My dad, William George Windsor, was born on March 6, 1898 in Kweiyang, Kweichow province. His sister, Joyce, was born a few years later.

Dad, who was generally known as Will, also attended Chefoo School. Following his graduation, he went to Toronto and worked in the Toronto Stamp and Stencil Company as a designer. His hand printing was artistic and beautiful.

Dad and Mother, of course, knew each other from their school days at Chefoo. They met again as students at Toronto Bible College, (TBC.) They renewed their friendship and soon fell in love. They shared the common bond of the call of God on their lives for missionary service in China. Where else? Dad's sister, Joyce, also attended TBC. There she met her husband, John Roberts, who became a pastor in Burlington.

Dad and Mother sailed separately to China, in 1921 and 1922 respectively. In those days, unmarried couples were required to finish two years of Chinese language study before marriage. Their wedding took place in Chungking, Szechwan province, on November 4, 1924. They were assigned to Kweiyang in the province of Kweichow, where Dad's mother was working. This was familiar ground for him. Dad writes the following in the *China's Millions* publication:

"We had been there scarcely two months when the request came from Shanghai to move up to Kiehkow (pronounced as Jeer Go). On our second night here, a band of 300 robbers visited us at half-past four in the morning. They fired several shots at our house and demanded entrance. They devoured everything edible in the house, wandered in and out of the rooms, helping themselves to things. They took our watches. Some of the people on the compound lost everything.

At the point of a pistol they threatened that if we reported their visit, or sent soldiers after them, they would come back and kill us. The Lord gave us peace in our hearts after the first fright, and wonderfully restrained the men from taking more of our things. One elderly church member died in their hands due to harsh treatment, and the soldiers demanded $1,000 for his body. We are looking to the Lord to bring blessing through this severe trial which the church is passing through." [2]

My dad travelled much of the time visiting little churches and Chinese pastors who needed encouragement. He rode on horseback along narrow paths, up and down hills, stopping to visit people of the Nosu and Miao tribes. They always gave him the best they could serve a visitor: mutton or ox, for every meal.

Once, due to the swollen rivers, he had to detour 60 miles, where it was usually only a 15-mile trip straight across. Dad wrote, "It is true we did not cover any great distance, only about 150 miles, but I assure you both horse and rider were glad when we reached home again." [3]

Dad occasionally had the companionship of another missionary or a Chinese friend. Sometimes, he slept in homes where people had typhoid fever. Only our Heavenly Father kept him from sickness. Mother was alone, sometimes for many weeks, while her husband was away. She managed the Mission Home with the help of Chinese servants. Eventually my dad became the Superintendent of the province, overseeing the work of the missionaries. This required much time away from home as well.

My parents had three daughters. Marjory Constance was born on May 28th, 1927 in Hong Kong. Why Hong Kong? A student uprising in south west China forced my parents and other missionaries, to flee to the coast. They arrived in Hong Kong around the time Mother was expecting her first child and thus, Marjory was born there. Eventually the missionaries were allowed to return to their respective areas to continue their work. So back to the beautiful hills of Kweichow went the new parents with their first born. Mother home-schooled Marjory until she was eight. Then they took her to the Chefoo Mission School. It would take approximately a month to travel the 1,000 miles from Kweichow in the south-west of China to Chefoo in the north-east.

Dorothy Joyce was born on April 21st, 1932 in Kweichow. This beautiful blue-eyed blonde, two-year-old died from dysentery on August 5, 1935, at Kiehkow, Kweichow. The baby's death was devastating, but having lost a child to this dreadful disease, mother was later able to comfort many Chinese mothers who had the same experience. This was a costly price to pay for being so far away from the homeland and proper medical care. I have a letter my dad wrote to Marjory. He said, "My, the house is too quiet with both of our girls gone."

With Marjory far away at school in Chefoo, it was a shock for her to hear the sad news of Dorothy's death so soon after saying good-bye to her parents. How she would miss her little sister!

It was six years later, when Marjory was 14, that Dad's fatal accident occurred. She does not remember having arms of comfort to surround her at this tragic news. She felt so alone.

Two years later I am sure that Marjory was happy to hear

some good news. For on August 1ˢᵗ, 1936 a third daughter was born in Chaotung, Yunnan, the province to the west of Kweichow. She was named Helen Jean, yes, that's me 'Made in China'.

Our close friends, Glen and Dorothy LaRue, were also stationed there. Dorothy helped with my birth. Forty years later, while in Florida, I met this couple. This was one of several "Surprise Gems" that God has given me during my life journey. Watch for them!

Chapter 3
"Oh Canada"

"Be strong and courageous. Do not be terrified;
do not be discouraged, for the Lord
your God will be with you wherever you go."
Joshua 1:9

I spent my pre-school years in the beautiful mountains of south-west China. My playmates were Chinese children. It was my privilege to have an *amah (*a nanny) who often took care of me. I remember drinking goat's milk, playing with my dolls and travelling from village to village by horseback or by sedan chair as my parents worked among the Nosu people. Gradually they made friends. They taught Bible truths and led people to put their faith in the Lord. Eventually small groups began to form, the beginning of small churches. Dad took many photos of these people, in groups and individually, identifying them with his artistic printing. Some have such radiant faces as new believers. He loved the children and they loved him.

Because of my dad's death in 1941, my mother left the duties of the Mission Home to join the office staff in Chungking, a densely populated city on a hillside by the Yangtze River in Szechwan province, about 200 miles north of Kweiyang.

I entered the temporary Mission School in Kiating, Szechwan, about 150 miles west of Chungking. I wasn't able to join Marjory at Chefoo in northern China due to the Japanese occupation there.

About 50 young children were enrolled in my school. Many of us had older siblings at Chefoo. Some of us were able to travel home for Christmas. The mode of transportation usually meant travelling by horse back, steamer boat or river boat. I definitely remember riding the rapids in a river boat (Junk) down the Yangtze — and being afraid.

During my three years in Kiating, we often heard sirens and had to hide in the air raid shelter at night. The teachers made sure we wore housecoats and did our potty thing in a hurry. In my childish mind, I was sure the enemy would spot my white house-coat and target us with their planes. By God's grace not one bomb fell on us.

Snakes and wild life were abundant. In the summer some of us slept on the balcony under our mosquito nets. The planes going overhead seemed so close. Fearfully I dug my face and hands into the bed clothes.

Different coloured balloons indicated the severity of the air raid. Red meant instant danger — head for the shelter. Orange meant a warning — be prepared. Green meant no immediate danger for the present. Certainly we heard the ominous sounds of the sirens as well. Once or twice I saw the balloons but the teachers acted accordingly for our protection.

During my time there, another worry left its mark in the presence of deep wells around the compound. I was terrified of falling into one. I now presume they were covered. This fear surfaced in many of my dreams later on in my life.

But there were positive sides to being in the Kiating school. I remember Sunday walks to the river and searching for tadpoles in the clear water. A prize catch was a dragon fly that I carefully held on my lap during a church service. Scripture memorization was a priority at the school. Our young minds were able to memorize Bible verses easily, including the whole chapter of Luke 2.

I will never forget watching the Chinese servants making

peanut butter on the grinding wheel behind the school. We enjoyed plenty of this item in our diet and to this day it is one of my favourite foods—unfortunately I'm not able to indulge as much as in those days!

Joan (Michell) Shortcliffe was my best friend. Her parents had worked with my parents in Kweichow. She lives in New Zealand, so it was a great surprise to meet her, along with her husband Jim, at a Chefoo reunion 40 years later in Toronto. Her brother, David Michell, was Home Director of the Overseas Missionary Fellowship, formerly the CIM, for Canada at that time. How delightful to recall our early days in China over a sumptuous Chinese feast. That was another one of God's "Surprise Gems" for me. Watch for the next one!

In the summer of 1943, my mother took me to the Mission Holiday Home up in the hills of Chungking in Szechwan. It was somewhat cooler there. In China, I experienced both cold winters and hot summers. Even on holidays, however, we had to hide in air raid shelters any time day or night when we heard the sirens warning of enemy planes coming overhead. In addition to the planes, I remember hearing wolves howling from a distance during the night.

When it was time for Mother to take a furlough, today often called home assignment, the war was still on. That created difficulties with travel. In March 1944, we flew on an air force plane from Chungking to Calcutta, India. I remember that trip. Metal seats lined the sides of the plane with luggage piled up in the middle.

The Burma Road, constructed in 1938, linked Burma (Myanmar) with the southwest of China. Japan's capture of the Burma Road forced U.S. Airmen to fly hundreds of missions a day into China in an airlift of epic proportions, including flying over the towering Himalayan Mountains. Pilots called this, "flying the HUMP." The HUMP was a pioneering aviation operation that had just about everything working against it: the foreboding mountains, the worst flying weather in the world, deadly Japanese fighters, the crudest of navigational aids, unproven aircraft, and inexperienced flight and maintenance crews. Military commanders considered a flight over the HUMP to be more hazardous than a bombing mission over Europe. More than 1,300 pilots and crew members were lost and more than 500 transport planes crashed trying to make it over the HUMP.

Going through the Himalayas was a rough ride to say the least, with most passengers getting sick. I did not, but to this day I have a fear of flying. I wonder if that trip had something to do with this.

Mother and I spent about three months in Calcutta waiting for a ship to take us to North America. Part of the time we stayed in a lovely hotel. The big ceiling fan in the bedroom really impressed me, especially since the weather was unbearably hot. I recall men who were called "Bearers" bringing us morning tea and bananas before breakfast. Walking the streets with Mother, however, showed me another side of the city. I saw so many desperately poor people.

Eventually Mother and I, along with a CIM family, set sail on the *Mariposa* for a dangerous voyage. It was still war time. The portholes had to be darkened at night so the enemy could not spot us. I can recall letting go of a balloon (why we were given them is beyond me) on the deck and being very afraid the enemy would find us and sink the ship, all because of me!

Each cabin had about ten metal bunks and required a good climb to the top one. The *Mariposa* stopped in Melbourne, Australia and Auckland, New Zealand. A ship steward bought me a much loved stuffed Koala bear. I treasured it all through furlough time.

We stopped in Buenos Aires, South America. Then our ship was pulled through the Panama Canal by mules—yes, real animals! On to Haiti, a port in Florida, and finally docking in Boston,

Massachusetts. From there we travelled by train to Philadelphia and on to Toronto in March, 1944.

This was my first time in Canada. I was eight years old. Mother and I lived for three years at the China Inland Mission Home at 150 St. George Street in Toronto. Mr. and Mrs. Brownlee, a dear gracious couple, were host and hostess at that time,

These three years of furlough included months of orthodontic work at the Medical Arts Building. Dr. Bliss always hugged me before working on my teeth. I also had eye surgery to try to correct a weak muscle in my left eye. That proved to be unsuccessful. We know now that this type of surgery should be done at a younger age. During my time at the Sick Children's Hospital, Mother brought me strawberries for a treat. I accidentally spilled them on the white bedspread. How humiliating!

I attended Huron Public School not far from the Mission Home. Here I was cornered against a wall by a classmate named Eddy and given a kiss. That was my first introduction to girl/boy stuff! Later, I was switched to Branksome Hall, a private girls' school. Maybe the kiss was the reason. Who knows?

Miss Lindsay and Miss McInnes were two Sunday school teachers whom I remembered well. They invited me to their homes and took me to the Toronto Zoo. My memory doesn't tell me which church we regularly attended, but I do remember the missionary conferences at the well known People's Church on Bloor Street, when Dr. Oswald J. Smith was pastor. Winter toboggan rides down the steep hills at Christie Pitts with other children from the Mission Home were fun.

Dr. Isaac Page, who held an administrative position with the CIM, was like an uncle to me. He and his wife, Mary, often invited Mother and me to their home. One Easter week-end, when staying there without Mother, I woke up to find a large chocolate Easter egg by my bed. What a treat!

Through the kindness of Misses Clarkson and Carpmael, dear

friends of my mother, I was able to go to Pioneer Camp near Huntsville in the summer. Here at the age of eight, as a "bunny" in the log cabin, I asked the Lord Jesus into my life with the direction of my cabin leader, nicknamed "Penny." She was from Pennsylvania, and I had the opportunity of meeting her again in Philadelphia not long after that.

During my three years in Canada I met my uncle on my dad's side, John Roberts and his five children for the first time, in Burlington. His wife, Aunt Joyce, was my father's sister. She died from pneumonia two years before my father's death. My cousins, John, Betty, Mary, Tom and Grace became like family to me. Mother and I saw them occasionally together, and I was allowed to visit them on my own in the summer. I loved the fun times with them. Although they were older than me, they took time to play house and have mock weddings in the garden. Grace and I played store, taking all the clothes out of the cupboard, putting them on the bed, and pretending to sell them to each other. Over the years, those cousins have included our family in many of their family events. I have been most grateful for their involvement in my life. Grace and I, now both in our 80's, share a special bond together.

On my mother's side, two of her brothers lived in Toronto. We often went to Uncle Jack and Aunt Mary's home for dinner. I still remember her delightful fried potatoes! When being driven home, I would sit in the front seat and ask my uncle to take us home the long way, just so I could stay with them longer. Uncle Alan worked at the Canada Life Insurance Company. I recall going to the company's Christmas party with Mother. I met Aunt Muriel and my cousins, Jerry and Tim.

Mother's youngest brother lived in Montreal. I clearly remember Uncle Gordon and Aunt Grace with their baby boy, John, visiting us at the Mission Home. I still keep in touch with cousin John.

Chapter 4
Meanwhile...Marjory

"Anything under God's control is never out of control." [1]

In December 1941 right after Pearl Harbor, the Chefoo School was interned, meaning they were confined until they were transferred to Temple Hill in Chefoo, the following November. This was considered a temporary measure, but they were now prisoners of war. The Japanese rounded up business people, Salvation Army members, CIM and other missionaries, children, and our grandmother on Dad's side.

My sister Marjory was among the group of students at Chefoo School. The Japanese forced 206 children and their teachers to leave Chefoo, which had been founded 60 years earlier. As they marched past the guards, they burst into singing Stanley Houghton's arrangement of Psalm 46.

God is our Refuge, our Refuge and our Strength,
In trouble, in trouble, a very present help.
Therefore will not we fear; Therefore will not we fear;
The Lord of Hosts is with us; The Lord of Hosts is with us;
The God of Jacob is our Refuge. [3]

In his book *A Boy's War*, David Michell wrote, "On the whole, conditions at Temple Hill for the first ten months were tolerable. While crowded conditions and lack of heating and sanitation were hardships, to be sure, the Japanese guards were not deliberately unkind."[4]

Then came the news that the Japanese authorities had decided all foreigners were to be moved one hundred miles inland, near the city of Weihsien. This meant a journey of two days and two nights by sea down the coast, and then a train ride. The children and teachers were assigned to the hold of the ship. There were no toilet facilities, but the teachers had expected this and provided each child with a potty.

After the sea voyage in which a lot of baggage was broken into or lost, the group was herded onto trains for a seven-hour journey. Upon arrival at the station, they had to march down a narrow, winding alley, through slum-like villages until they arrived at high walls and two wooden gates. Over the gates was the inscription: "Courtyard of the Happy Way." They had arrived at Weihsien Concentration Camp. It was September 1943. Each prisoner was given a number written on an arm band. Roll call for 1500 prisoners was twice a day; no one could leave until everyone was accounted for. Porridge was made of black bread. Lunch was stew, possibly made of horse meat. Supper consisted of leftover ground up stew. A teacher knew growing children needed calcium. She taught them to grind egg shells to swallow with water. The only dessert was shortbread, with the sugar and butter given by the Japanese.

Each prisoner was required to work; Marjory was part of the kitchen duty, which included serving the prisoners their meals. Bed bugs and rats were prevalent; no proper toilets were available; and the primitive showers had no curtains!

The Chefoo teachers worked hard to run a school. There were no textbooks and little paper. Marjory wrote a math assignment on toilet paper, then lost it! But the Oxford School Certificates were miraculously found in time for graduation. Amazingly, the students who graduated had the equivalent of first year university.

The teachers had done so well with so little.

Marjory became ill with typhoid fever. Because of the lack of facilities, she was isolated along with a nun, in the morgue, of all places! Due to her illness, she lost a year of school. Many people prayed for her and for all those held as prisoners. Fortunately, one of the teachers came everyday to check on Marjory and attend to her needs.

A special visitor who risked his life to see her was Eric Liddell, the man who refused to run on Sunday at the 1924 Olympics. He is featured in the *Chariots of Fire* movie. Marjory remembered him speaking so kindly to her. She said, "I can still see his face standing over me." Marjory called this her "brush with greatness." He was so great as an athlete, missionary, and humanitarian. At age 43, Eric Liddell died from a brain tumour just a few months before the war ended. He left behind a loving wife and three small girls who had been sent to Canada for safety. Marjory had an opportunity to meet his widow and children after the war.

In July 1944 our elderly grandmother, Annie Windsor, died. She had previously spent much of her time running an orphanage during her years in Kweichow. Her wish was to spend her retirement years at Chefoo by the sea but this was cut short, due to the imprisonment at Weihsien.

Friday, August 17th, 1945 started as an ordinary day but ended in an extraordinary way! The American military flew over the camp in their B-2 bomber planes, letting down seven parachutists. One of them was even a former Chefoo student! They risked their lives and became heroes, for the Japanese could have shot them. All the prisoners cried, shouted, and screamed! The Salvation Army band played especially prepared national music. Outside the camp a market was set up where old clothes were exchanged for apples and eggs. They were free! I still have the arm band Marjory wore, as well as a bright silk piece of parachute material.

Later, the American military put the North Americans on a

troop ship with 300 marines. They stopped at Pearl Harbor and had their photo taken with the Red Cross personnel who had kindly given them new outfits to wear upon release. Miraculously the clothes fit them beautifully. After landing in San Francisco, many, including Marjory, were taken to Vancouver and then to Toronto.

By this time, Marjory was eighteen years old. She moved into the Mission Home where Mother and I had already been living for two years. Marjory had her own room on the top floor. It had been seven years since mother and I had seen her! We certainly had a time of getting re-acquainted, but it was too short a time to bond as a family. Marjory went to a local college to learn secretarial skills. Two years later, Mother accepted an office position back in Shanghai.

Chapter 5
Slow Boat to China

"What God allows may hurt you, BUT it will not harm you"[1]

In November 1948, with our trunks packed and name tags on all my clothes, Mother and I travelled by train to New York City to sail for Shanghai. We boarded the ship and settled into our cabin. Before the ship left the dock, however, Mother took ill, suffering from a nervous break-down. This, in part, was due to the stress of preparing to leave for China. We couldn't proceed to sail. Mother was able to phone the CIM Mission Home in Philadelphia. Mr. George Sutherland, affectionately called "Uncle George" by almost everyone, came to take us off the ship. Mother was taken by car to Toronto, where she spent a full year recovering.

During this year, I lived with Roger and Mary Howes, the CIM Home host and hostess in Philadelphia. They took me into their hearts and home. Their two daughters, Mary Ruth and Flora Nell were like sisters to me. I look back on my year at 235 W. School House Lane with fulfilling and enjoyable experiences. Yes, I did miss my mother. The details of my mother's time in Toronto are not in my memory, but I knew she was being well looked after, in the Women's College Hospital. The CIM family in Toronto were there to support her as well.

Mrs. Howes taught Flora Nell and me to crochet around handkerchiefs. A trip to New York city to see Radio City, the Empire State building and climb up the Statue of Liberty were highlights of this year. It was my privilege to attend the Quaker School during which time I first heard Malott's tune of *The Lord's Prayer* which continues to be so meaningful to me. I took piano lessons from Mary Ruth's organ teacher and enjoyed playing those pieces until in my late seventies. It was at Christmas I first heard "O Holy Night" sung by Flora Nell's school choir. These are all wonderful memories for me. I loved my year in Philadelphia! How gracious my Shepherd was to provide me with the perfect home allowing me to function happily during my mother's illness. Happy memories of this year obliterated any negative aspects of this time in my life.

Another one of God's "Surprise Gems" was to unexpectedly meet Mary Ruth 55 years later at a Toronto Chefoo Reunion. We were both under an umbrella in pouring rain fumbling with coins to pay the parking fee. Look for the next "Surprise Gem."

Marjory was attending Gordon College in Boston so she was able to join me for Christmas in 1948. During my year in Philadelphia it was my privilege to meet Isobel Kuhn, CIM missionary to the Lisu people in south Yunnan, China. She is the author of 15 books.

When I was 12, with Mother having recovered, we packed another set of trunks. I don't know what happened to our first set. We took the train across Canada to Vancouver. I delighted in that trip, especially peeking out the window in my bunk at night watching the Prairies fly by. To this day I have a passion for travelling by train, but not by plane as previously mentioned.

From September through November 1949, we stayed in the Vancouver CIM Mission Home waiting for a ship to take us to Shanghai. Mr. and Mrs. Eldon Whipple were the host and hostess of this lovely home. I recall other missionary children being there as well as the Whipple children. I remember taking piano lessons there. That's an effective way to keep children out of mischief. Also for several hours a day, Mother taught me the basics of

French, Math, and English money denominations, (pounds, shillings, and pence in those days).

In November we boarded the *Islandside*. This freighter carried four big boilers and sixteen small aircraft, as part of the freight on deck, also twelve missionaries and two children. Had we known how difficult the voyage would be, I don't think any one of us would have set foot on the gang-plank. But did the apostle Paul know how dangerous some of his trips would be? Sometimes obedience involves a risk.

As the ship lifted anchor, I remember the missionaries on board along with those on the wharf singing Joseph Hart's song. It is one of the most loved and often sung hymns in the CIM:

> How good is the God we adore,
> Our faithful, unchangeable Friend!
> His love is as great as His power
> And knows neither measure nor end!
>
> 'Tis Jesus the First and the Last,
> Whose Spirit shall guide us safe Home;
> We'll praise Him for all that is past,
> And trust Him for all that's to come. [2]

The sailors were a tough lot, and the Pacific Ocean was mercilessly rough. The ship's cook broke his hip due to a huge wave that knocked him over while he walked the deck. The *Islandside* rolled so much we had to stuff the dresser drawers with toilet paper to keep them from falling out. Near the end of the voyage the steward announced that there was no paper left!

Once a sudden lurch of the ship brought a pot of hot soup onto Mother's lap. I remember the salt and pepper shakers rolling off the tables scattering onto the floor in the dining room. Most everyone was terribly sick (again, not me). Mother's friend, Betty, recited the following;

> "There are three stages of seasickness;
> I'm afraid I'm going to die,
> I wish I could die, and
> I'm afraid I'm not going to die."

Yet, CIM missionary Mr. Rhodes bravely went down into the hold to encourage the sailors and tell them about God's love. I must have exasperated my mother, for on this trip I got the last spanking of my life. Perhaps I misbehaved because there was so little for children to do. The adults wisely held many prayer times for safety during the storms.

Crossing the International Date Line made us miss Christmas Day, but that did not stop the sailors from celebrating. Our French steward dashed around the halls removing fire axes from glassed in cupboards, afraid that drunken sailors would do damage to each other and the ship. He also hid the knives from the galley. We were told to stay in our cabins with our doors locked and not to open the door for anyone.

I can't help but think of the verses that David declared in Psalm 107:28-30: "Then they cried out to the LORD in their trouble, and he brought them out of their distress. He stilled the storm to a whisper; the waves of the sea were hushed. They were glad when it grew calm, and he guided them to their desired haven."

The 50 memorable days on the Pacific Ocean finally ended when we arrived in Kaohsiong, Taiwan. The crew unloaded the airplanes which had been heavily damaged by the storms.

Our ship had to stay in port an additional two weeks, and we were not allowed to go ashore. I am not sure why. Probably it would take that much time to unload all the damaged freight before sailing the final stage up to Shanghai.

At last we got off the ship. Mother was back in her homeland, the country of her birth. China was always home to her. She settled into the secretary's flat at the Mission Home at 1531 Sinza Road in Shanghai. She was truly happy to be back amongst her missionary family. As well as doing secretarial duties, she was the "Recorder" for the mission. That involved listing where each missionary was from, their qualifications, next-of-kin, where they were currently, when they went on furlough, when they came back, dates and names of children's births, when their passports expired, and so on.

Early in 1950, I returned to the CIM school. Every school was called "Chefoo," no matter where the location. My school this time was located at Kuling in the valley of the famous Lushan Mountains. To get there, I along with six other children escorted by a teacher, flew two hours by plane to Kiukiang in Kiangsi. That brought us to the foot of the mountain. We began to climb up the steep mountain, 4,500 feet above the plain. Young children and older adults were usually carried up the steep mountain in sedan chairs. These are chairs made of cane slung between two poles and carried by four coolies. Two are in front and two behind. Our luggage was carried in a similar way. It was about eight miles up the mountain which included climbing up the "Thousand Steps." This term was symbolic for a long stretch of steps at one point on the climb. The edges of the path seemed to swing over the cliff below. The climb took three hours. Along the way, we stopped at a tea house, called *t'ing-tze* (decorated pavilion) for rest and refreshment.

I am thankful for my memories of Kuling. It was a blessing to have attended this era of the Chefoo school. At most there were 130 children plus teachers and support staff. Situated high up in the breathtaking mountains, it is often described as "Heaven on Earth." The CIM's magazine, *China's Millions* described Kuling as "...the freedom of the hills, the lure of the mountain streams, the wealth of flowers, the rare moths and beetles, the haunts of the birds, the exquisite beauty of the frozen mist on tree or shrub, the glow of sunset behind dark mountains..."[3]

The name Kuling, a play on the word 'cooling' (from the heat of the Yangtze lowlands), was not a Chinese word. It was designated by Westerners at the end of the 19th century.

Winter was a fairyland of ice and allowed for great toboggan rides. Spring produced wild azaleas on the hillsides and the sound of cascading water down the stream. Summer meant hearing the cicadas chirp and enjoying a pleasant visit with friends at Fairy Glen (a holiday resort nearby). Autumn brought the breathtaking colours of the trees. It was truly a God-given paradise.

In addition to the beauty of nature, I remember that Saturday morning was "Sweet Day." We lined up to receive candy from our own tins, candy our parents provided. (I carried on this tradition with my own children.)

On Sunday afternoons, we rested, wrote letters to our parents, and took walks to exotic spots such as the Three Trees, Lion's Leap, Monkey Ridge, Land's End and the Temple in the Clouds. The weekly Sunday evening Hymn Sing was special to me. We sang from the *Golden Bells* hymn book, and the songs took a firm root in my heart. I was not the only child who shed tears from homesickness as we sang.

Although the school high up in the mountains seemed isolated from the world, we had Boy Scouts, Girl Guides, Cubs, and Brownies. Our Girl Guide and Brownie leaders, Miss Phare, Miss Elliott, and Miss Young inspected our patrols each week, making sure our uniforms were in perfect order. The Guide patrols were named after birds. I belonged to the Redstarts and will always remember my leader, Eleanor, a gentle and kind older student from the U.S.A.

At Easter one year, the school performed John Stainer's *Crucifixion* in the old stone Church of the Ascension, which was Anglican/Episcopal. The experience of singing under the direction of our Principal, Stanley Houghton, impressed me so much that I had a copy of this cantata in our piano bench for many years.

For Christmas holidays I joined others as we rode the train for two days to Shanghai. You can imagine how excited I was to see Mother again after a year of separation! Not all children were fortunate enough to travel home because their parents lived too far away. "Home for Christmas" meant living in the secretary's flat with my mother and having my very own room. It was delightful to be spoiled by all the "Aunties" as the lady missionaries were called, and by my mother as well.

Mother and I took the rickshaw (a two-seater chair on wheels pulled by a man generally running) into the busy streets of Shanghai for shopping sprees. I had to get new clothes made for the next school term. On school days the girls wore a navy tunic and white blouse.

The train trip back to school took two or three days. En route we stayed at Chinese inns and ate delicious meals followed by using the customary piping hot white cloth to clean up. The heart-wrenching good-bye from Mother was almost more than I could bear. For several nights I cried into my pillow hoping no one else heard me. As with many MK's, we put on a brave face during the day but the tears flowed freely at night. Now I realize that my heavenly Father was caring for me even then.

On July 17th 1950, our beloved principal, Stanley Houghton suddenly died from a heart attack, while he was playing tennis. We gathered together that evening in the Assembly Hall to hear the news from vice-principal, Gordon Martin. Mr. Houghton was remembered for his love of children and his musical abilities. He composed the music for the song based on Psalm 46 which was sung during the internment of the Chefoo School, previously mentioned.

While at Kuling "puppy love" surfaced. We both knew it for sure, as we shyly cast glances at each other in passing. We communicated only by writing notes to one another, passing them with the assistance of his brother, during assembly study time. The irony of this first "love" was that he took top honours the day marks were read in assembly. I lay shattered at the bottom of the class! I ran back to the dorm in tears from this humiliating experience. How I would have loved to have had an older sister or teacher to console me.

Upon returning to Canada three years later, the "puppy love" turned into friendship. After occasional outings together, we went our separate ways. I highly respected this young man.

My most treasured memory from the three years at Kuling was my friendship with Margaret Pearce, a classmate whose parents were our school doctor and nurse. We loved talking and walking together. She excelled in sports, Girl Guides and art. Our friendship has continued all our lives. You will meet her again later in the journey.

Kuling days were happy in spite of some rough spots, especially the academics. It is frightening to contemplate what might have happened if I had remained in such a demanding British educational system. The Oxford exams would have overwhelmed me. My Heavenly Father had lovingly planned the next steps of my life.

Chapter 6
Adventures of a Teenager

*"When our confidence is in God
we may rise above circumstances."*[1]

By 1951 the threat of Communism was rapidly becoming a reality. My school had to be evacuated. I, along with several students had already gone to Shanghai for the Christmas holidays. It was decided that we, accompanied by a few staff members, would go to Hong Kong. Those still at the school in Kuling, would join us later. The mission headquarters in Shanghai was to be closed with only a few staff remaining, including my mother. I was 14 at this time, and yet again, I had to say good-bye to her.

With some teachers and several children, we took a train ride from Shanghai to Hong Kong. For three days and three nights, all we could do was to look out the big train windows and watch the mainland of China become part of our past. Some of us would never return. This was our last time to see the familiar sights of China such as temples, pagodas, rice paddies, and fields of tea.

When we arrived in Canton, China's most southern border, each person and each piece of luggage was roughly inspected by guards on the station platform. Every item was put on display.

Finally we crossed the border, over the bridge into Hong Kong, a British Crown Colony. This was free territory. My life in China was over.

Our school was given eleven old metal army buildings, called

Quonset huts. They sat on a derelict piece of land behind a crematorium on Chatham Road, but only yards away from the China Sea. It was called "Freehaven," a place for evacuees coming from China. This became our home from January to August. We continued our schooling after the rest of the students arrived from Kuling in April. Before that, I vaguely remember going to a British school carrying our wicker baskets full of books.

My Hong Kong memories, however, include having lunch in the luxurious home of Mr. Braga, the business man who was instrumental in getting the Quonset huts for the school.

Routinely we saw beautiful sunsets over the ocean. One particular sunset was so bright with red and orange hues that my friends and I decided the Lord was coming to take us to Heaven that night!

I remember visits to Tiger Balm Garden – an exotic tourist attraction. We met missionaries coming out of inland China. Many of them had gone through harrowing experiences under the pressure of the Communist regime. Some were parents who were more than glad to be reunited again with their children.

One night during my time in Hong Kong, my mother still in Shanghai, suddenly became ill with a bowel obstruction. The mission hospital had been closed except for bare essentials. My mother, with intravenous tubing in her arm, had to be carried on a bed across the compound. Her life depended on the skill of the Chinese Christian surgeon who "happened" to be available then. He found her bowel was gangrenous. The mission arranged a prayer alert to be sent to missionaries and supporters in the homelands. While my mother's desperate condition was being announced to everyone in the dining room in Hong Kong, a kind teacher "took me out for tea." She explained to me what was happening to my mother in Shanghai. This kindness saved me having to hear the news in front of everyone. God graciously restored my mother to good health.

Eventually she and the remaining missionaries left Shanghai for Hong Kong. I vividly remember her crossing the bridge from China into free territory. We were together once again! We lived in a Mission apartment on Nathan Road for about three months — a precious time, but all too brief.

Eventually every missionary was evacuated from China. Stories of this massive withdrawal of over 800 personnel are nothing short of miracles of how the Lord provided money and accommodation. One outstanding example is the rental of the two Shanghai Mission buildings to a hospital connected with a military commission. The mission received three-years' rent in advance for the buildings! God provided this money to pay for all the travel expenses of the missionaries leaving China and arriving safely in Hong Kong. How our wonderful Shepherd provided for His many sheep!

When it became impossible for missionaries to return to China, the Mission moved their Headquarters to Singapore in South-East Asia. Several of the missionaries returned to their home countries to be with their families. Others felt led to continue their work in new countries in Asia. The China Inland Mission (CIM) now became the Overseas Missionary Fellowship (OMF).

Mother was asked to join the office staff in Singapore. That meant I would return to Toronto, Ontario, Canada to finish my schooling. This was the most severe separation I experienced, for it meant saying good-bye, not only to my dear mother yet again, but also to my best friend, Margaret Pearce. She returned to England with her family. Eventually her parents made their way to Singapore. I shall never forget that heart-wrenching farewell at the Hong Kong airport. Every time MK's move, it seems that they leave someone or something precious behind. On this trip I travelled with a family and two single missionary ladies, and I carried my own passport. The following is taken from the tiny diary in which I wrote as a 15-year-old:

"Took off a 9:30 am Monday, August 6th, 1951. Sunny day. Wonderful view. Read. At 1:30 lunch served with sandwiches and tea. Passed through many clouds, very rough (maybe that's another reason that I don't enjoy flying). *Slept. Quite cold, needed a coat. Arrived in Bangkok. Ate at restaurant: two courses, ice-cream and tea. While eating heard the song, "Show Me The Way To Go Home" on the radio. Took off for a five-hour flight to Chittagong, East Pakistan. Felt rotten. Lights put on about 9:45pm HK time. Landed in Lahore, West Pakistan. Too rough, felt rotten. Plane plans changed consistently. Took flight at 10-ish to Calcutta. One engine had to be repaired. Taken by bus to a posh hotel and fed a meal, filled out papers, and shown to our rooms.*

We had breakfast of figs, eggs, a roll and tea. Back to our rooms for a Quiet Time with God. We ate meals at very odd hours, talked with pilots, went to a museum. Took off again. Fifteen minutes into the flight the pilots realized they had forgotten the log book, so had to turn around, land again, then take off for Karachi, West Pakistan."

We continued to land and take off at Bahrain, Damascus, and Rome. We flew over Cyprus and the Persian Gulf. Over the Alps we found it so cold, that the stewards kindly gave us blankets. Finally we arrived in Antwerp, Belgium, and had to switch planes for London. I wrote down every item that was served to us from the whole trip and realized we were fed extremely well, even if breakfast was at two in the morning!

One of the missionary ladies, Miss Blott, escorted me by bus to the CIM Mission Home in Newington Green, London, England. I was shown to a small bedroom on the top floor and told what time I needed to appear for the next meal. Such a feeling of loneliness and homesickness embraced this shy 15-year-old, seemingly all alone in a strange country.

I wasn't completely alone though. My mother's cousin, Jean Austin, took me to places of interest such as Buckingham Palace, Hampton Court, and Windsor Castle.

At the Mission Home bookstore, I bought a book that became one of my favourites: *Treasures of the Snow* by Patricia St. John. Immersing myself in the life of a little girl in the Swiss Alps certainly helped me to feel much less alone during the week in London. I gave this treasured book to one of my granddaughters, Sarah, when she was 15 years old.

An American couple whom I met in Shanghai, and again in England, accompanied me on the voyage from Southampton, England to Halifax, Nova Scotia. I believe this couple wanted to "adopt" me but my mother wasn't giving me away. She also preferred that I live in Canada, and not the U.S.A. The Atlantic crossing was smooth sailing compared to the rough voyage on the Pacific ocean four years previously.

Mother had instructed me to write down all my expenses. In my diary I noted $2.85 for a sandwich at the Halifax wharf, 40 cents for two boiled eggs in Montreal, and $2.00 for tips on the ship. Looking at this, I realize I didn't record everything. I know I wrote some post cards to my mother and friends in Hong Kong. They cost three cents each!

The American couple continued to escort me on the train from Halifax which arrived in Toronto on August 24th, 1951. Mr. Bill Tyler met us at Union Station and drove us to the Mission Home.

It is marvelous to think of how my Heavenly Father provided for my next home. I became the "adopted" daughter of Bill and Vera Tyler, the host and hostess of the CIM Mission Home at 150 St. George Street. They lovingly took me into their hearts and home. I shared a bedroom with four-year-old Maybeth for the first year. Gordon was eight years old and John was just a baby. They nicknamed me "Honey," a name they still use today.

The Mission Home, acquired in 1927, had many luxurious features. I can still picture the tall windows that looked out on beautiful trees, the large dining room able to seat 30 guests, two sitting rooms at the front, the stained glass window at the top of the main stairway, and the butler's pantry between the dining room and kitchen. Nineteen bedrooms accommodated retired workers, missionaries on furlough, families, and other guests. The house also had ten fireplaces, seven or so offices, and a large meeting room. Such indelible memories I have of the four years I lived with the Tyler family. They truly gave me a "Home within a Home."

Returning to Toronto meant I was able to see my sister Marjory more often. How special it was to have my older sister live in the very same city! She had graduated from Gordon College in Boston and was now on staff with the Inter School Christian Fellowship (ISCF).

For my first year in Canada I lived with the Tylers and attended high school at Branksome Hall, a residential and day school for girls. I was extremely fortunate to attend this school, no doubt through the kindness of Miss Edith Read, the principal, who took a special interest in girls from missionary and ministerial backgrounds.

For my second year, I became a boarder, living in residence Monday to Friday. On the weekends I took the street car back home, where Auntie Vera gave me a room of my own. On Sundays, I took the street car again across the city to Calvary Church, the church that supported Mother while she was overseas.

Branksome Hall gave me wonderful experiences. It was a school with strong Scottish traditions. We wore the kilt and tie of the Hunting Stewart Tartan with a green blazer. This tartan is "worn by the Queen when she is "off duty" and during moments of relaxation."[2] What an honour it was to be chosen as a Prefect. For my two years as a Prefect, I had extra responsibilities such as ringing the morning wake-up bell, taking attendance for the compulsory pre-breakfast walk around the block, and other duties. The Prefects wore the kilt and tie of the Royal Stewart Tartan with a red blazer. "The Royal Stewart tartan is the best known tartan of the Royal House of Stewart, and is also the personal tartan of Queen Elizabeth II."[3]

One year I was the Chieftain of the Douglas Clan, one of several Clans. We held our banners up and marched to the sound of bagpipes for special occasions.

Each morning at breakfast, Miss Read read portions of the Bible to us. We memorized long passages of Scripture and were rewarded with prizes, usually a Bible or a special book.

Invitations to concerts were posted on the bulletin board, and we were expected to reply formally on good note paper. We learned how to master Scottish dances and along with the boys of St. Andrews College, performed them at the Granite Club in front of city dignitaries and people from the upper class. Was this the same shy teenager that came from China?

It was also my special joy to sing in the choir and to compete in the Kiwanis Music Festival at the Eaton's Auditorium. I remember the year when we won top honours. My knowledge of the Scottish traditions increased as we celebrated the birthday of Robert Burns, a Scottish poet born January 25th, 1759. We watched Haggis, the national dish of Scotland, being ceremoniously carried into the auditorium. It is composed of liver, heart, and lungs of a sheep and mixed with beef, oatmeal and seasoning. This mixture is packed into a sheep's stomach and boiled. I like sheep, and I like oatmeal but not packed and mixed up in this manner. Oh help!

It was my privilege to be the president of the Inter School

Christian Fellowship (ISCF) group. This included the frightening task of making announcements about upcoming meetings in front of the entire school during assemblies. This led me to depend on the Lord as never before. I still felt somewhat alone and knew it was necessary to lean hard on my Good Shepherd for His help.

In 1953 the well-known Christian Dutch woman, Corrie ten Boom, came from Holland to North America to tell of her experiences in the Nazi concentration camps. She, and some of her family members, were imprisoned for helping many Jews escape from the Nazi Holocaust during WWII.

Miss Read invited her to challenge our small ISCF group. I remember sitting on the floor by her chair, awed by what she had gone through. Hearing Corrie ten Boom speak was another privilege of being at Branksome Hall at the right time. As my sister Marjory had "her brush with greatness" with Eric Liddell in their concentration camp, meeting Corrie was my "brush with greatness."

A Branksome Hall teacher, Mollie Brien, became my friend. She let me use her bedroom for my Bible Study preparation, giving me a quiet get away from the dorm. She always left Peek Frean cookies on her desk for me to enjoy. How could I resist?

I stayed an extra year in school to obtain my Grade 12 diploma in preparation for nursing school. Entering Branksome Hall upon arriving from China, I had been placed in the Home Economics course and received my diploma for that as well. Graduation ceremonies in June 1954 were memorable with bagpipes playing, and girls wearing long white dresses carrying dozens of red roses. I was honoured with three prizes, certainly not academic! They were for Loyalty, Integrity, and Music Appreciation. Auntie Vera and Uncle Bill attended the service. They were always there for me, supporting me during the ups and downs during high school days. But at graduation, and many other times, I missed my mother who was overseas the entire time, except for one brief furlough. I knew, however, that I could ask my Heavenly Father to help me when faced with difficult situations.

Each summer during my high school years, I went to Pioneer Camp in Muskoka near Huntsville. This camp was run by the Inter Varsity Christian Fellowship (IVCF). The boys, girls, and junior camps were situated on Lake Clearwater. These summers at Pioneer were, without a doubt, the happiest months of my life up until then. I was seldom just a camper. I worked to pay my way by being part of the kitchen help. I, known as "Smiles," along with my girl friend, known as "Chuckles," spent hours and hours peeling carrots and potatoes. We had days off for fun, including swimming, canoeing, and campfires.

My sister Marjory, nicknamed "Chee Chee," (Chefoo school) was a leader for many years. That meant we happily saw more of each other. Marjory, and maybe others, introduced to Pioneer Camp the same uplifting chorus based on Psalm 46 that they had sung as prisoners. We sang it for many years. One summer when Mother was in Canada, she helped in the camp office. She was given the name "Windy" (Windsor). How special to spend a summer with her, no doubt, arranged by the Camp Director and the mission, for me. The Camp Director, Cathie Nicoll, also attended the Chefoo school in China. "Nikki" as she was called, had a tremendous influence on young people. She worked with IVCF for over 50 years. She was highly respected and given several honours in her lifetime including the Order of Ontario.[4]

Pioneer Camp will always hold a special place in my heart. As campers, we looked forward to getting into our pyjamas and housecoats and hurriedly getting a good spot by the campfire with our leaders. We took overnight canoe trips on Mary and Fairy Lakes, pitching camp on small islands even when it was pouring rain, our heads under the canoes with ground sheets covering the rest of our bodies! There is nothing more picturesque than a bright red canoe on a Muskoka Lake! At camp we slept in tents with the flaps up all summer (except for storms). We sang wonderful songs such as *"Land of the Silver Birch,"* and *"On the Shores of Lake Clearwater."* We also had good food.

Most of all, I learned to have a deeper appreciation for the Lord God, our Creator. How nostalgic it was to attend the 70th anniversary of Pioneer Camp in 1990, to sit by Clearwater Lake, to enjoy lunch, and to visit the Bunny cabin where I made the decision to accept God's gift of eternal life as a young girl of 8 years. Lo and behold, another one of God's "Surprise Gems" turned up. My beloved teacher, Mollie Brien, from Branksome Hall, was there. I had not seen her in 45 years!

Connie Windsor
– Helen's mother

Will Windsor
– Helen's dad

Marjory – age five

Dad and Mother travelling

Helen – age two   *Dorothy – age two*

Travel by sedan chair

Helen beside her sedan chair

Travel by sampan on the Yangtze River

Helen with amah (nanny)

Marjory age 14 at Chefoo

A Thousand Steps

Helen first time with Marjory
at Chefoo

Americans liberating POW

Quonset huts in
Hong Kong

Dining room in
quonset hut

Chapter 7
Milestones

"For I know the plans I have for you…
plans to prosper you and not to harm you,
plans to give you hope and a future."
Jeremiah 29:11

Following high school graduation and my final summer at Pioneer Camp, I left the Mission Home on St. George Street. I moved in with John and Edith Bell at 46 Gormley Avenue in Toronto. John Bell was Deputation Secretary, now called Mobilization Department, of the CIM. Edith was known for her wonderful cooking as well as being a good Bible teacher. This was a busy home with comings and goings of their children, including Ruth, who lived in the States, and Mary, Ken, and Dorothea. One or more boarders like me also lived in the home. Boyfriends came to visit. Grampa Bell, well into his 80's and also living there, loved to tease us all during our courting days. He always kept an eye on the road waiting for the next young man to arrive. He usually sang, "The Camels are Coming, Hurrah, Hurrah!"

I lived with the Bells, and also worked at the Bell Telephone Company. I needed to pay my board and also save for nursing school. A straight run on the Yonge Street subway from home to work was handy. I was grateful for the father of one of my school friends who procured the not-too-demanding job for me. His daughter, Wanda, had cerebral palsy, and I had been able to help her in school, especially writing her notes.

In the spring of my final year in high school I met Walter Glen Dancy at Calvary Church in Toronto. His father, Harold Dancy was participating in the Missionary Conference. When Walter entered my Sunday school class as a visitor, we both noticed one another. Unknown to me at the time, Walter was sure he had found his girl, and it was me! Certainly this tall, handsome, blue-eyed blonde, and dark-suited young man carrying his Bible caught my attention as well.

During the next few weeks I saw him from a distance until we landed up playing basketball on opposite teams during an ISCF social event. What match was I at five feet, for this six foot opponent? This never to be forgotten day was April 8th, 1955. Oddly enough, 51 years later on the exact same date, at the age of 69, in a granddaughter's school gym, I scored four baskets in a row!

Our first formal date was the spring banquet with ISCF. I had several suitors that spring. Aunt Vera tells me she was watching the buds opening but only one opened completely: Walter. I am thankful that the Lord chose a mate with a similar background as mine. Walter was born in Jos, Nigeria, on December 18th, 1935 six months before me. His parents were missionaries with SIM then known as the Sudan Interior Mission. In 2000 the name was changed to Serving In Missions, still SIM.

Walter's father, Harold Dancy was the mission's builder. That meant the family moved to many different areas. Missionary life was not easy. Did God promise it would be?

Walter, along with his three older sisters, Betty, Gladys, Evelyn, and younger brother, Arthur, spent all of his school life at the Gowan's Home for missionary children located in Collingwood, Ontario. The school was a memorial to Canadian, Walter Gowan, one of three men who organized SIM in 1893.

How Walter ever got through school is a miracle as his mind

was on sports, especially football, all the time. He played very well. His passion for football and sports in general continued throughout his life. Years later, Walter stated that if he could live his life over again, he would make three changes: more study, more sports, and more dates! Oh, Oh!

In September 1956 through the influence of Cathy, a friend from Pioneer Camp, I entered nurses' training at Toronto East General (TEGH) and Orthopedic Hospital on Coxwell Avenue near Danforth Avenue, East Toronto. For the next three years, I lived in the nurses' residence with 53 classmates. I always went to the Bells' home on my days off.

I'll never forget my first few days in training. Like some others, I was scared of the unknown. Waiting for me, however, was an encouraging note from a dear friend, Gertrude Seaman. She was a former missionary who now cared for missionary retirees. She had three daughters in nursing, so she understood my feelings.

My three years in nursing school were challenging for me academically. I had to study hard and long to get passing marks. I entered nursing because I wanted to take care of sick people. The most rewarding aspect, therefore, was spending time at the bedside of my patients, trying to make them more comfortable and attending to their needs. Some events stand out in my memory: giving my first practice injection to a classmate and dissolving into tears afterward; having to stand on a stool in the operating room to assist with kidney surgery, because of my being so short; and missing most of my three month rotation at the Hospital for Sick Children due to having a bad infection that required me to stay in the Sick Bay at our residence. I had to make up this time on our own hospital's pediatric ward.

Two of Walter's sisters were nurses. Betty worked in my hospital's nursing office as an evening supervisor. I was happy to chat with her from time to time. Gladys was at Victoria Hospital

School of Nursing in London at the same time as I was in Toronto. The Dancys' home was only a few blocks away from my hospital. I don't remember that this had any bearing on my choosing to study at TEGH! I do remember many lovely Sunday dinners in Walter's home when I was off duty or on evening shifts. Walter was my tower of strength. He always encouraged me to keep going. I often dreaded facing a new ward but with my confidence in God, Walter's support, and the prayers of my family, I was able to make it through.

During the seven years of high school and nursing school, two friends of my mother's, Agnes Carpmael and Amy Clarkson, sent me five dollars every month. With this money I was able to purchase toothpaste, nylons, and other necessities. Regretfully, I neglected to thank them in a timely manner. These dear women also attended my graduation and later hosted a bridal shower for me. By then, I habitually wrote thank-you notes promptly and was grateful for their continual kindness.

I enjoyed the friendship of the Nurses Christian Fellowship. This included city wide socials. One year I was elected NCF President of my hospital. I found this leadership role rather daunting, but it was a good experience for me.

During my third and final year of training, my mother returned from Singapore. With her permission, on March 16th, 1959, Walter asked me to marry him. This was no surprise to anyone. We had been dating for over four years. We celebrated at a Swiss Chalet restaurant that evening.

Four months later brought another exciting event: Graduation Day on June 6th, 1959. I clearly remember a day with clear blue sky, white crisp uniforms, and bouquets of red roses. Smiles on the faces of the class of '59 said it all. I was deeply thankful Mother was there to see me graduate. Friends and family who had supported me so much were also present. Along with my diploma, I received the KST Award. Again, this was not an academic award. It stood for Kindness, Sincerity, and Tactfulness. My teachers and classmates put my name forward. I was humbled with this honour. It seems my Heavenly Father blessed me in spite of all my struggles in various classrooms over the years.

After graduation I spent my days and evenings studying for the Registered Nursing exams in August. This was no easy task during the summer months especially since I was still at the hospital until October making up for sick time.

Mother had been staying at the Mission Home. After I wrote the exams, she left for her next term in Singapore. This was another good-bye with tears, but the thought of marrying Walter took away some of the sting of separation.

One day during the fall while on duty, we learned that the entire class of '59 had passed their RN examinations. Had I heard correctly? Indeed I had! You couldn't have found a more thankful girl. I know it was God's goodness to me, for the required amount of studying had overwhelmed me. With my RN status a reality, I worked in the newborn nursery at TEGH for the next few months. I was back living with the Bell family. Early morning walks through the park in the dark to catch the subway were a bit unsettling. Again I realized God's care and protection.

The following year, on March 5th, 1960 Walter and I were married at Calvary Church in Toronto. It was a cold but joyous day for us. We were fortunate to have an outstanding wedding party consisting of loyal friends, as well as my sister Marjory and two of Walter's siblings, Gladys, and Arthur. However, the cloud hanging over the day was that my mother could not be with us. We wired a bouquet of flowers to her in Singapore. She received eight different kinds of orchids in the arrangement. The ceremony and reception were taped for her. Mother's greetings to us came in the form of a wired cablegram which Uncle Bill Tyler read: "LOVING CONGRATULATIONS HELEN WALTER REJOICING WITH YOU IN THOUGHTS AND PRAYER

GREETINGS APPRECIATION TO ALL PRESENT MOTHER
COLOSSIANS 1:18B"   In those days cablegrams were printed
in full capitals.

In contrast to the expense of today's weddings, I rented my
wedding dress. I had it for only three days! Mary Bell loaned me
a head piece and veil from her recent wedding. My bridal bouquet
consisted of a little white Bible that Gladys loaned me from her
wedding to Bill Carey the year before. It was covered with minia-
ture pink roses and white ribbon.

Vera Tyler and Edith Bell gave their time and love to help
make this day special for us. John Bell walked me down the aisle.
I will always look back with much appreciation for the three
bridal showers and the many wedding presents we received. So
many people were kind to the little bride whose mother was so
far away.

The choice of a honeymoon destination may have been un-
wise. Nevertheless, we now have a "I can't believe we did this"
story to relate and pictures to prove it. At -20 degrees F, we
drove to the Bells' cottage in Haliburton on the day after the wedding. What a picture we made, pulling our toboggan over ice-
covered Gull Lake with luggage and a record player! Then we
had to dig our way into the cottage with the help of a nearby
farmer. To get water we had to dig a hole in the ice on the lake.
After the challenge of lighting a fire in the stove, eventually we
enjoyed some hot chocolate. We put on layers and layers of
clothes, and of course we had "our love to keep us warm!" We
stayed only one night at the cottage. I think a course in wilderness
survival should have been a prerequisite for this honeymoon!
The next day we checked into the Tally Ho Inn near Huntsville
for the remainder of the week. I believe it was Charles Swindoll
who said of his own honeymoon: "It was a colossal comedy of
errors!" We were in good company.

By the time of our wedding, Walter had received a two-year

Diploma from Central Baptist Seminary. He was working at the T. Eaton Company in downtown Toronto. I was enjoying working in the nursery at East General Hospital only five minutes away from our apartment on Monarch Avenue. Mother and Dad Dancy lived ten minutes from us and we loved having them over for dinner. Life seemed pleasant.

Within five months all this changed. Walter was asked to transfer to the new Eatons Store in London to help open the shoe department in the new mall. I hated to leave the precious newborns, and the familiar surrounding of friends, church, Mother and Dad Dancy, and my sister Marjory. On the other hand, it was a new adventure for a newly married couple.

Chapter 8
Setting up a Home

*"Each day of our lives we make deposits
in the memory banks of our children."*[1]

Our first home in London was a one-bedroom apartment at 107 Grand Avenue. Walter's sister, Gladys, and her husband Bill Carey lived one floor below us. Gladys was well gifted: she received her ARCT diploma (Associate of The Royal Conservatory of Toronto), attended Central Baptist Seminary in Toronto—the first woman there to receive a Bachelor of Theology degree, received her RN diploma in London, and became an accomplished artist. She was chosen as valedictorian for both graduations. Wow!

Bill was transplanted to London at the age of 14. His father, William G. Carey, at age 45 felt the Lord's call to give all he had to serve Him. He resigned his teaching position in New Jersey, where he was known as an outstanding pianist, organist, and music teacher, to be Director of Music at the London Bible Institute. In London, Bill enjoyed sports, playing the trumpet and participating in Christian young people's activities. He graduated from South Secondary School, London Teachers' College, University of Western Ontario, and eventually University of Toronto where he received his Master of Education.

While completing his BA, he met Gladys Dancy at Wortley Baptist Church. After a two year courtship, they were happily married on June 26th, 1959, (a year before Walter and me). They settled in at 107 Grand Avenue.

Bill and Gladys warmly welcomed us to London. Their church became ours. Wortley Baptist had many young couples and this was good for both our spiritual and our social growth.

I found a job just a 15-minute walk away at Victoria Hospital. The ward to which I was assigned catered to people of influence with each patient having a private room. Their demands became increasingly difficult. I soon transferred to Westminster Veterans Hospital where Gladys worked. This was a more relaxed atmosphere, and I liked caring for the men who had served in various wars. As nurses, we wore white muslin veils similar to army nurses overseas.

On November 16th, 1961 at Victoria Hospital Brian James was born by Caesarian section after a difficult labor. I had loved working with newborns as a nurse. Now, we were overjoyed to have our own. Not long after coming home from the hospital, I heard Brian choking in the night. As his face was turning blue, I instantly turned him upside down to dislodge the mucous from his throat. What a frightening experience for a new mother, yet I had done this many times in the newborn nursery. I have always felt that the Lord used my hospital experiences to give me the confidence needed for motherhood. Before that, I had little exposure to babies or children.

One week prior to Brian's birth I passed my Driver's Licence test in our little green Volkswagon. Walter was so proud of me, especially considering the shape I was in! Getting my licence enabled me to use the car for doctors' appointments, shopping, and working nights occasionally.

We often visited Mother and Dad Dancy in Toronto with "Baby Boo" (my sister's nickname for Brian), cradled in the back window, a practice unheard of today!

Lorraine Ruth was born on August 27th, 1964, also by Caesarian section. Walter had taken little Brian to stay with my cousins Mary and Stirling Cantelo in Burlington. He then went on to Toronto for a brief visit with his parents knowing Lorraine was to be delivered the next day. But she surprised us by arriving the previous evening, so Walter didn't get to see his daughter until midnight. I was awake for the C-section, a unique experience. Tears of joy and happiness flowed. To think that we were blessed with a darling two-year-old boy and a precious little girl. I couldn't have felt better during both pregnancies. I was never sick, just full of expectations! How blessed we were. Baby showers were not common at this time, so I was amazed at the kindness of family and friends in providing us with much appreciated baby gifts.

I stopped working during the second pregnancy. We knew it was important for me to be home full-time.

Walter wanted to be more creative in his work. Selling ladies' shoes didn't meet that need. He left his job at Eatons. Through Bill Carey's influence, he began a new job at Ideal Monuments on Springbank Drive. Walter found the creative and physical aspect of the work rewarding. In addition, the new job led him to become a skilled craftsman in granite and stone. With the kind help of Walter's boss, Lloyd Rapson, we were able to purchase our first home at 58 Albion Street. It was an older house with a big back yard, where Walter made an exceptional ice rink. This attracted many neighbourhood children in the cold winter months. We did our laundry in the kitchen with a wringer washing machine that we moved in and out each wash day. Brian and Lorraine slept in bunk beds in one room. Later we added another bedroom with the help of friends. Dad Dancy, a former builder, came to help, too.

We will always remember our dear neighbours, Fred and Daphne and their three children: Angela, Michael, and Lesley. Fred was a cabinet maker, and he redid our kitchen cupboards. I learned many things from Daphne who was an example of a good wife, mother, and homemaker. Our children played well together and attended Empress Public School. Miss Cook was Brian's first grade teacher. She was noticeably caring and spent individual time with her pupils.

Those were busy years raising a young family. At times we did not have a car and had to rely on church friends for rides. We appreciated their kindness and later, when we did have a car, we were happy to give people rides when needed.

Walter walked to work two miles each way. This kept him in good shape. He also worked many hours overtime to meet expenses, so I would not have to return to nursing. I enjoyed being home with the children, sewing dresses for Lorraine, mending, cooking, and baking from scratch, as well as entertaining. My strong desire to be a full-time homemaker, I believe, came from my not growing up in one place. I had moved from here to there throughout my childhood. Maybe I felt that I needed to actually get nested in one place. By saying this, I don't regret for a minute my experiences in many homes and boarding schools. I wouldn't have missed living with the Howes, Tyler, and Bell families for anything. I never resented my past. In fact, my life was enriched by having cross-cultural experiences and now, you are reading about them.

In addition to being busy at home, we both taught Sunday school at Wortley Church and worked on a number of committees. For several years we also hosted a monthly CIM meeting to pray for missionaries overseas. The children were well behaved and accepted being in bed with their books by the time the guests arrived. Most Sunday evenings after church and bedtime stories, we played classical music as well as gospel songs while the children fell asleep. Doesn't this all sound so serene? A change was coming.

In September 1971 Walter was offered a job in Cannington, near Lindsay, as a brick layer. He liked working in the monument trade but was always ready to try something new. Our cousin Don Perkins was the pastor at Cannington Baptist Church. We rented our home in London, bought a half-ton truck, and rented a new home on an acre of land in Argyle near Beaverton.

This was the beginning of an unforgettable year for our family; great fun for the children, but not so much fun for their parents! On the plus side, we had the freedom of the country, trees to climb, woods to explore, bus rides to the one-room country school, and visits to the old country store where Mrs. Fleming kept anything and everything a person might need. That store was more interesting to browse through than many museums.

People at the church were friendly, and we enjoyed corn roasts and social times together. It was great to have our cousins, Grace and Don and their children close at hand.

The down side of living there was the dangerous winter driving, the well water running dry, the odours coming from the animal slaughter house not too far away, and the long overtime hours Walter had to work. One time when Walter was cutting the lawn, a sharp metal piece pierced into his leg causing it to bleed profusely. Up until then, I had never driven our new truck. Now I had no choice. I drove Walter to a doctor in a nearby town. The doctor didn't believe anything was in his leg. However, when Walter went to work the next day, the pain was excruciating. We headed back to the doctor. I asked him take an x-ray which clearly showed a rusty nail measuring one inch and a half, embedded in the calf of his leg! The nail was removed.

After this incident, we found it necessary to find another doctor. It was our delight to find Dr. Dick Vinden who was attending our church and had been a Chefoo MK in the same school and internment camp as my sister Marjory! Could this be called one of God's "Surprise Gems?"

That winter of 1971, I insisted on driving seven-year old Lorraine into Cannington to watch an evening ice-skating performance at the arena. On the way, I popped into Mrs. Fleming's store to get a jug of milk. She couldn't believe we would try such a trip when snow was falling so heavily. But I was determined not to disappoint Lorraine. It was tough going through the snow, nevertheless, we arrived safely. Driving home, however, I couldn't take the usual road due to the foot or so of snow that had fallen during the evening. I tried another road, only to find ourselves getting deeper into snow with blizzard-like conditions all around. I thought it best to return the way I had just taken. In order not to get stuck, which might have been fatal, I ever so gradually inched my car around using the stick shift back and forth and praying very hard that we wouldn't get stuck. My worst fear was to be caught in this snow storm in the middle of nowhere with my little girl. I could not see any lights around and the reserve gas tank in the Volkswagon was indicating low.

The next day was Sunday, and I had planned to teach Psalm 23 to my Primary Sunday school class. Right now it was important to apply the truths of this Psalm to myself and to Lorraine. I talked to her about the Shepherd who always watches over His sheep. I don't know if that helped her, but I gained comfort from this fact, as opposed to the thought of making newspaper headlines: "Mother and daughter found frozen to death in blizzard!"

With great relief we found our way back to Cannington. I knocked on the door of our friends, George and Sheila. They welcomed us warmly into their home. We had met this kind and caring couple at the church, and became close friends. They always went the "extra mile" with their God-given gift of helping others.

We phoned Walter to see if he and Brian could make their way into town, but that was impossible. Can you imagine how thankful we were for a warm bed and caring friends following our terrifying experience!

Oh, our Good Shepherd was certainly protecting His sheep

that night! Sometimes sheep can be so prone to wander and find themselves in such trouble. I happen to be one of them! I don't remember if I got to teach the lesson on Sunday or not. Maybe so, for our church was just a few blocks away.

During our year in Argyle my best friend, Margaret Pearce, came from England to stay with us for three weeks. She is the one I had said farewell to in Hong Kong 20 years earlier.

A few pages back, I said you would meet her again. Upon leaving China, she completed high school at a Christian boarding school in North Wales. In the next 20 years she gained the following qualifications: SRN — State Registered Nurse, SCM — State Certified Midwife, MTD — Midwife Teacher's Diploma, and HV — Health Visitors Certificate. Also, during those years Margie attended Capenwray Bible School, and spent one year as a midwife in The Nazareth Hospital, Israel. Later she entered Hospice work, caring for terminally ill patients and their families. Always caring, loving, and meticulous in everything she undertakes, she is my life- long God-given best friend.

The original plan was that Margie would be with us in London. In the meantime, however, we had moved. We were not in the most ideal setting to entertain such a special friend. Those who know me understand I do like things to be done "decently and in order." In any case, we welcomed Margie to country life in Canada. She thoroughly enjoyed the beauty of our Ontario autumn with the colours at their best. While the children were at school, we took long walks discovering different paths into the forests which were ablaze with colour, a paradise for taking pictures. We took trips to Niagara Falls and London on two weekends. On her third weekend, a classmate from China days, Grace (Glazier) Bryer, came from Wheaton, Illinois, to join us. I remember thinking how unique it was to have a trio made up of American, English, and Canadian women. We spent a lot of time reminiscing about our school days in Kuling. In spite of running out of well water, Margie had a refreshing three week holiday with us. Watching her plane take off from the Toronto airport seemed more than I could bear and the tears flowed freely—so reminiscent of the farewell in Hong Kong 20 years earlier.

Chapter 9
The Shepherd's Plan

*"However dark the **nows** may be in your experience,*
*the **afters** of God are worth waiting for!"* [1]

Walter's job with the brick layer ended early in 1972. The work was just too strenuous and demanding, although anyone who knew Walter well, knew that he wasn't afraid to work hard. For a few months keeping bread on the table was a challenge. We will never forget the kindness of the church family who lovingly provided us with food and some temporary work.

Psalm 50:10 became a favourite Bible verse for us: "He owns the cattle on a thousand hills." We often sang John Peterson's song with those words as we drove past hills along the highways. We remember friends, such as Roy and Bonnie, and George and Sheila, who walked with us through this difficult time.

Walter returned to the work he knew best. After buying an air compressor, he began doing cemetery inscriptions under the name of Dancy Memorials. This brought in good pay but required Walter to be away from home for days at a time, leaving me alone with the children. For one week that summer Brian and Lorraine went to camp in Muskoka, and I was able to travel with Walter.

By the end of the summer we had sold our London home and purchased a home in Peterborough, not far from Argyle. I think we had had enough of country living. I was pregnant, but the very weekend we moved to Peterborough, I unfortunately miscarried. Our faithful Shepherd knew what lay ahead for our family.

Brian and Lorraine began their school year in Peterborough in September, 1972. We were excited about our new home at 1396 Hawthorne Road. Walter built a fireplace in our recreation room, and also built one for a neighbour. We entertained a lot, mostly company from London.

We soon became members of Ferndale Bible Church. The children took part in Pioneer Clubs, Boys Brigade, ice skating, hockey, accordion, trumpet, and piano lessons, as well as earning pocket money by delivering weekly flyers to homes.

After three years at Hawthorne Road, we moved to a smaller home at 1602 Cherryhill Road within walking distance of the church. Brian especially liked his new high school at Thomas A. Lucas Secondary and Lorraine adjusted well at Kawartha Heights in grade six.

In the early spring of 1976 I had abdominal surgery. By God's grace, I recovered in time for the family to join our cousins, Mary and Stirling Cantelo and their daughter, Connie, on a trip to Florida. This was the first time our family had gone on a holiday trip, although we had previously spent time at various cottages. We had a wonderful time including days on the beach at St. Petersburg, and a visit to Disneyland. Walter and Stirling's humour kept us well entertained. As we got back into the van after finishing a meal in a restaurant, the men would ask, "When do we get to eat next?" This was repeated after every stop. What fun!

We also visited Glen and Dorothy LaRue. These retired missionaries had worked alongside my parents in inland China. Dorothy was the nurse who attended my birth. They had kept in touch with my mother during the intervening years. Remember the first "Surprise Gem"?

Walter was working out of town most of the week. How we looked forward to the weekend with him. He was really too busy.

One day while finishing up an inscription, one of his legs just wouldn't move at all. He had to crawl to the truck. Somehow he managed to drive home.

I had just had another surgery. I was forced to forget about myself, however, and the next week was a blur of caring for Walter. He had to take seemingly countless medications for relief of the pain in his leg. Following a week of this, I took him to the Emergency Room at the Civic Hospital on a Saturday night. The next Monday, Walter had surgery to remove the ruptured fifth disc in his back. That had been the cause of his severe pain. His sense of humour was evident as he played a few tricks on the nurses, but he recovered well. How thankful to God we were for the quick diagnosis and treatment of this injury. But, of course, Walter needed time for his back to heal.

Now we were "up against a brick wall" in more ways than one. Walter had already begun building a three-foot high brick wall as an embankment to our sloped lawn by the driveway. The project was not safe to leave unfinished for too long. During the week that Walter came home from the hospital, our neighbours across the street entertained relatives from England. Amazingly enough, they were brick layers! They saw the unfinished project and kindly completed the wall free of charge. I am still in awe of this — another miraculous provision provided by our loving Shepherd. What could be more exciting than that!

Disability insurance helped us with the basics of living. Being newly self-employed, however, we were not fully aware of compensation coverage. Walter felt he could not engage in heavy work again, so he sold the business van and equipment. This was not an easy decision to make, especially for a family man in his mid-forties. At times we felt numb as if we were falling off a cliff or sinking to the bottom of the ocean. I do not think the children realized this as we tried to keep as normal a routine as possible. But we do remember Brian offering to give us some of his paper carrier money which, of course, we declined. Such a thoughtful teenager.

It is a blessing that at the time of our surgeries, hospitalization, and job losses, we were so aware of the goodness of our Heavenly Father. Friends were wonderfully caring. Our church family overwhelmed us with their gifts of love, money, flowers, dinners, groceries, baking, visits, and often treats for the children. I clearly remember one Sunday when Paul and Andrea, children of our friends, gave us two dollars from their allowance.

When Walter's back was stronger, he began to look for a job. The only work he could find was repairing recreation rooms. This was a part time job so the disability income was cut off. Walter also ventured into selling life insurance for a time. This was not his niche, and it did not meet our living expenses. We both put out applications for work in spite of our numb state of mind. Sometimes we must be brought to the end of ourselves and to the bottom of circumstances in order to fully prove what God's resources are. Our faith was stretched to the full as we asked Him to show us what we should do next.

Again, as we had in Argyle, when we were in the car, we would sing, "He owns the cattle on a thousand hills." We responded, if God can provide for the cattle, He can provide for us, as well.

Promises from the Bible gave us hope. We learned that God allows our adversities to filter through His fingers of love first, and that He is still with us no matter what. The devotional book, *Springs in the Valley,* by Mrs. Charles Cowman was our constant source of strength. My mother wisely gave us this book. It had been a comfort to her over the years and now became our treasure.

To be perfectly honest, I need to say that in the business of working hard, raising a family, and even keeping busy working in the church, (all of which are good in themselves), we took God's blessings for granted. We neglected to daily fine tune our relationship with Him. We didn't take time to read His words of wisdom and comfort and talk with Him in prayer. We didn't ask for His direction as the day began. Our bridge to God had weakened. We needed this stormy experience so we could learn anew the importance of a closer walk with God. Three words from *Springs in the Valley* devotional say "Prize your storms!" Oh yes? Now with all the props gone, we were totally dependent on Him.

With no definite work in Peterborough on the horizon, Walter inquired at Ideal Monument Works back in London regarding re-employment. We spent a weekend in London to confirm the job, now under a new owner, and to arrange for housing. Back in Peterborough, we put the 1602 Cherryhill house up for sale. It sold in a week. The garage sale that followed was difficult, as we had to part with household goods and precious mementos. This move, however, gave Walter and me hope—a chance to earn a wage again, even if it was minimal. Hope is a precious gift to keep us from losing heart completely.

This move was devastating for both children as they had to say good-bye to their church and school friends. Brian was 16 and Lorraine was 14. Our hearts were torn for them. We knew they were happy at their respective schools and church. Why did they have to go through what I had experienced so frequently in my childhood? I'm sure it was a strengthening factor for them in the long term. It enabled them to adjust more easily to new situations, as it had done for me.

Ferndale Bible Church gave us a meaningful farewell on our final Sunday by presenting us with a wall clock and a monetary gift. They also gave us friendship and lasting memories. What a precious church family we found them to be. Fred and Ann are our friends to this day. They are a couple with the gift of helps. I still keep in touch with Sharon, another sweet friend.

Fortunately, we qualified for government assistance, as our move was out of town. We packed everything that was left after the sale, including a much treasured picnic table. When we arrived in London on March 22, 1978, to our surprise we were informed that a charge of $300 would be levied to cover the weight of the picnic table. We didn't know whether to laugh or cry. Our church had generously given us a departing gift of $300 just two days before! We expected to use that for groceries, but now we had to use it to pay for the extra weight. How special to own a picnic table that increased in value from $25 to $300! We were amazed, yet thankful, at God's provision and timing through all this.

For the next two years, we lived very simply as we began to rebuild our lives at 471 Berkshire Drive. For the second time in our lives, Bill and Gladys welcomed us to London, and we began attending our former church, Wortley Baptist.

Our next door neighbour turned out to be the niece of a missionary whom Mother and I knew from our days in Shanghai. What a coincidence! Agnes and Stuart became good friends over the years.

I remember feeling sorry for myself on our first Christmas back in London because we had no carpet. Then I remembered that our Lord didn't have a house with a carpet, let alone a home at all, and I was at peace.

Fortunately for Lorraine, she found a close friend, Liz, in grade eight and we became friends with the family.

Eventually, in the fall of 1978, we began attending West Park Baptist Church. This was a smaller congregation where the Youth Pastor, Dave Peterson and his wife, Carol, gave all their energies to the young people. We well remember Scott Strople from the Youth Group, who went out of his way to make Brian feel at home with the boys his age. We, as well as our children, felt most comfortable under the leadership of Pastor Paul and Vi Fawcett at West Park.

I began volunteering at Victoria Hospital in the hopes of eventually securing a job there. That didn't happen, so I brushed up my typing skills at night school and found a temporary job with Key Property Management for a brief time. When West Park Church needed a secretary, I applied for the position and got the job. In fact, I was the first woman to work in the new church office. I enjoyed being the receptionist and appreciated the opportunity to work with the pastors. The job was both challenging and delightful. As summer approached however, I decided to resign so that I could be at home.

Brian, then 17, found part time work at the Kensal Rental shop next to Ideal Monuments. Job opportunities, both full and part time have always been available to Brian. His work ethic and pleasant, conscientious manner contributed to his success. We are humbly proud of him.

Both children deserve special recognition for their loyalty to us during this Spartan time in our life. I don't remember either of them complaining or asking for spending money even when their more affluent friends could buy snacks or go out to eat.

After two years at the Berkshire townhouse we moved to 1220 Royal York Road just five minutes walk from our church on the corner of Royal York and Hyde Park Road. This proved most helpful as both children were involved in opportunities at church with the youth, music, and sound system.

This delightful townhouse, with a fireplace, was our home for 15 years. There we entertained friends, missionaries, and held anniversary and wedding celebrations.

Each Christmas was extra special since we looked forward to seeing the "red army" arrive in London. This needs an explanation. My mother, my sister Marjory, her friend Miriam, and sometimes her sister Elsie, would all turn up wearing red coats. Why? It wasn't planned; they all happened to buy red coats at the same time! Such fun we had over this. No one who knew "Aunt" Miriam will forget her love for children. Sending a stick of Wrigley's chewing gum in every birthday card was her specialty.

Both she and Marjory gave generously to our family in many ways, as long as they were able.

For 25 years on Christmas Eve when Walter finished his work, he went the "extra mile" by driving to Toronto to bring Mother, and sometimes Marjory, to London for Christmas. They felt safe with Walter at the wheel in spite of the many times that the road conditions were most unfavourable.

My mother had left Singapore in 1967 for retirement at age 67. It was always easy to remember her age because she was born in 1900. She lived in the CIM Toronto Mission Home for several years prior to moving to Fellowship Towers, on Yonge Street. She came by train or bus to visit us for a few days occasionally. She was a delight to have and many times we would be in gales of laughter over almost anything! She spent most of her time with us washing dishes or doing the family mending – and such meticulous mending she did! While the children were at school she and I would enjoy a "cuppa" downtown together.

Marjory and Helen – sisters together at last

Bill & Vera Tyler at Helen's high school graduation

Mother, Marjory and Helen -first time together after the war.

Helen dressed in Hunting Stewart kilt and tie.

Helen's nursing graduation

Walter – seminary graduation

Walter and Helen's wedding – March 1960

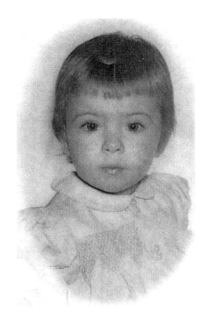

Brian – pre-school   *Lorraine – age one*

Our young family

Chapter 10
The Empty Nest

"Courage is the willingness
to step into the unfamiliar,
and then to take another step[1]

This stage in life comes only to other parents, or so we thought. Brian graduated from school and found work to earn his board and keep. Eventually he moved from our home to his own apartment. As his mother, it was hard to see him go, but I also realized it was time for him to make his own life. We were honoured that Brian was our son. He was a caring, thoughtful, fun loving young man who loved the Lord.

Lorraine graduated from high school and worked awhile before going to Moody Bible Institute in Chicago. The time at Moody was a learning experience for her as well as for her parents. We enjoyed several trips to see her. When we said goodbye to Lorraine for the first time, the "tables were turned." For the whole of my early life, it was my mother who was leaving me. I faced the separation from a young girl's view point. This time it was my husband and me leaving our young daughter behind. As the tears flowed, Walter and I both realized for the first time how difficult it must have been for our parents to leave us behind at boarding schools and mission homes. Lorraine enrolled in the music programme but didn't feel suited to the course. She decided to return home after the first semester and entered London Baptist

College, receiving a one year diploma at the end of that school year.

Lorraine worked at several secretarial positions, each job coming to her easily as was the case with Brian. Her various jobs all gave her good experience. Along with working, she was heavily involved in the music at church. For several years Lorraine was the accompanying pianist for West Park's annual Living Christmas Tree performance under the direction of Charlie Loshbough. Charlie made a deep impact on Lorraine and gave her the foundation for future ministries. Later while in her 40's, Lorraine earned her ARCT music diploma, as her Aunt Gladys had done many years earlier.

With Walter's skill and the knowledge of the monument business, he felt led to strike out on his own again. While pondering this change we came across a verse in Job 19:23,24:

> Oh that my words were recorded,
> that they were written on a scroll,
> that they were inscribed with an iron tool or lead,
> or engraved in rock forever.

This unusual prompting from the Scriptures helped to confirm our decision to re-establish Dancy Memorials. This was a step of faith. For the first year we worked with the Horta Craft Company owned by Jim and Les Lofgren from our church. We shared staff and most importantly, they got us established in bookkeeping skills, for which we will always be grateful.

The Lofgrens moved elsewhere and by August 1979, we were on our own. We decided to move the business across the street. One week later, a tornado hit southwest London demolishing most of the roof tops in the industrial district. The building we had just moved into was left untouched! We were amazed, but also so thankful for another evidence of our Good Shepherd's protection.

On our business card was the motto: "a family business that cares." Walter was known in the monument trade for his excellence in working with granite. Countless times he went the extra mile in order to meet the customer's wishes, sacrificing himself for a deadline. Each customer was important to him, allowing for friendly chats. Brian worked many years with Walter in the shop. He had a skill for chiseling on stone, and along with Walter, produced many beautiful memorials for our customers. He was most loyal and dedicated. Not wishing to take over the business, however, he left for other employment at a local cemetery.

Over the years we employed several young men and women, including Lorraine, who helped in the office for several months while she established her own business giving piano lessons. I worked full and part time, also as secretary and bookkeeper. Later, we were privileged to employ Margaret Norman who had immigrated from England with her family. She became a valuable employee, taking on the bookkeeping as well as sales. Margaret endeared herself to the customers with her warm and caring manner. We could not have managed without her commitment to Dancy Memorials. Her daughter Sarah assisted in the office as well.

Through the music programme at West Park, Lorraine met Jim Drennan. He was attending London Baptist Bible College (now Heritage College and Seminary.) After completing a Theology degree, he graduated with a Masters in Christian Education. Jim and Lorraine married on July 2, 1988. Two years later Jim accepted a position as Associate Pastor at Oxford Baptist Church in Woodstock. At that time, my cousins, Don and Grace Perkins served as pastor. Lorraine continued to teach piano.

Two years later on September 29, 1990, Brian and Christine Redman were married, having met through the youth group at church. Christine is a Registered Practical Nurse and worked part time at a nursing home connected with St. Joseph's Hospital in London.

Both children's weddings clearly honoured God as they made commitments to each other with a desire to build Christian homes. We are now blessed with four lovely "children" who love the Lord. Both couples had two daughters: Sarah and Hannah (Jim and Lorraine), Rachel and Michelle (Brian and Christine).These girls have brought much joy to us as grandparents.

My mother had been living in the Shepherd Lodge nursing home in Toronto for several years. On the morning of May 22, 1992 we received a call to say that Mother was not responding although she had been alert the day before. Walter and I arrived and a few hours later she died peacefully at the age of 92. She had been able to see only one of her great granddaughters, Sarah, at age six months when Lorraine brought her for a visit.

Although separated from my mother for many years, I always knew I was loved. She wrote weekly letters and sent yearly birthday parcels from overseas. I knew I had a praying mother, a very disciplined mother, and a mother who sang the old hymns as she made her bed each morning. The tragedies of life did not make her bitter. Abraham Lincoln once said; "No man is poor who has a godly mother."[2]

In my heart, I was not truly prepared for her death. I had so much I still wanted to ask her, especially in the light of attempting to write my life story. As mentioned, the early years in China had not been easy for Mother and Dad. However, Mother believed in the God of the Impossible and many events in her life strongly enforced that belief. Her firm faith and close walk with the Lord left a deep impact on my life. Her early morning rising with a cup of tea, to be still with God, is my daily practice, too.

About the time of my mother's death, I became interested in sheep, especially as I read Phillip Keller's book, *A Shepherd Looks at Psalm 23*. It was fascinating to learn the ways of the sheep and how the shepherd cares for them. I really took to the idea of God as our Shepherd, and I learned how He cares for us,

His sheep. Many times we get off the right path and have to be brought back by the Shepherd's rod of correction, but always in a loving manner. It was so comforting for me to know that my Shepherd cared for me, even though I sometimes acted like a wayward lamb. I often read a chapter of Keller's book before falling asleep at night. It has a calming effect.

Collecting stuffed sheep and ornaments became my hobby, and it wasn't long before my family and friends helped to enlarge my family of sheep. Some of them even came from England, Scotland, and Paraguay. I often find ways of sharing about God's love to others, as I talk about my love of sheep.

Walter and I referred to our four granddaughters as "our little lambs." We told them about the Good Shepherd who cares for His own little lambs as we cuddled babies and toddlers, along with stuffed sheep and lambs. Rachel, Sarah, Michelle, and Hannah are grown-up now, but in my heart they are still my little lambs. It is a joy to look back on the days when we played dolls together and had "tea parties on the ceiling" as in the Mary Poppins' story. What fun it was to tuck them into bed and read stories with them in our guest room made just for little girls. Walter's aunt, Charlotte Dancy, gave us the following poem;

Why God Made Granddaughters

God must have patterned granddaughters
From angels up above,
And sent them to grandparents
To cherish and to love.
They have smiles as warm as sunshine,
And brighten any day
By being so delightful
In such a charming way.
And whether they are very small
Or lovely grown up misses,

They keep grandparents happy
With loving hugs and kisses.
Yes, God created granddaughters
Because He knew they'd be
The dearest, sweetest blessing
He could give a family.[3]
Author Unknown

In January, 1993 we moved from our town house on Royal York Road to 803 Valetta Street, in a well established subdivision not far away. We were thrilled to purchase a home again. It was such a sweet little one-floor bungalow with a huge back yard. Naturally the granddaughters loved this home. They had plenty of room for hide-and-seek both inside and out. They could also play soccer, our family's favourite sport. Occasionally, I took one or more of the granddaughters to the nearby park to fly my kite as I helped them hold onto the string. I especially liked flying the kite when the wind was strong. The following poem explains why:

Riding the Wind
"We were never intended to be buried by our apprehension, earthbound by the weight of worry...
I have learned to release the heaviness of
my anxiety into stronger,
more capable hands.
When I do, it is as if I ride the wind!" [4]
Author Unknown

The family surprised Walter with a party to celebrate his 60[th,] birthday, a week before the actual date, December 18. We had a light supper at a restaurant, after which I suggested we get back home since a friend was coming to see us. On the way home I gave Walter a mint to suck – or so I thought. Actually it was an estrogen pill! Oops! He spit it out mighty fast, you can be sure. The party guests certainly had a laugh at this oversight on my part. Walter's sister, Gladys, created a memorable cake. It was a completely detailed football field much to Walter's delight. Chocolate, of course!

Six months later I walked into our office with a camera focused on me. Why? Walter and his secretary, Margaret, then proceeded to tell me that they had already arranged for my dear friend, Margie, to arrive in two weeks from England as a special present for my 60th birthday!

This was one of God's biggest "Surprise Gems" ever! I was so surprised that my face reflected shock more than surprise. This didn't fulfill their photo expectations at all. We were busy the next few days preparing for this unexpected but most looked-forward to visit. It had been 20 years since Margie had last been to Canada—those memorable three weeks in the country up north in Argyle.

This time the one-week visit was all too short, but it gave us time to catch up and deepen our friendship which has survived mostly through letter writing and telephone calls since our school days in China. The one flaw in this visit was that Margie's luggage did not arrive until three days before her departure. Margie has been experiencing increased loss of vision, but we are grateful for e-mail which she still enjoys, as well as telephone calls.

About this time we were pleasantly surprised to find out that Aunt Vera and Uncle Bill Tyler (my guardians during high school in Toronto) had moved to London. They lived only a few blocks away from us. Their reason for moving was to be nearer to their own family members. They attended our church and were much loved by everyone. This, indeed, was another one of God's wonderful "Surprise Gems" for me along my life's journey.

Chapter 11
New Beginnings

"The contents of any cup can be transformed when we see that the Hand holding it is that of the Father."[1]

Time brings changes as we all know. It was not easy for Walter and me to see Jim, Lorraine, Sarah, and Hannah move to Ottawa in the spring of 2000. Jim accepted a pastoral position at Alta Vista Baptist Church. His parents lived in Ottawa and were not in good health. His father, Bill Drennan, died not long after their arrival. It was good that they were there.

The family became involved in church and community activities. In addition, Lorraine taught 25-30 piano students in her home. We were able to make the seven-hour drive and visit them from time to time. We enjoyed sightseeing at some of the points of interest in our nation's beautiful capital. We could do this because our capable office administrator, Margaret, managed the business in our absence.

By March 2003, the big back yard at 803 Valetta Street became too much of a burden for Walter to care for, since he was also carrying a heavy load in the business. In addition, he was diagnosed as having silicosis. This is a lung condition caused by the inhalation of silica dust, which was used in the early days of sandblasting. It is not used today. We knew a change was necessary. In the early months of 2003 a friend sent us this Bible verse, Isaiah 43:18, 19, which in the Good News Translation reads:

"The Lord says, Do not cling to events of the past or dwell on
what happened long ago.
Watch for the new thing I am going to do.
It is happening already—you can see it now!
I will make a road through the wilderness
and give you streams of water there."

We had no idea what this meant at the time, but we had an inner feeling that it was significant. In February, Walter suggested moving to a condo, where he would have no outside responsibilities (cutting grass was very irritating to his breathing). Through the influence of our friend, Roy Wallace, a retired SIM missionary from Africa, we viewed a condo at The Gainsborough and knew it was for us. We made a down payment with the condition that our home would sell within six weeks.

The Gainsborough is ideally located at the corner of Wonderland and Gainsborough Road. It is situated on five acres of lush landscaped grounds. Shopping, grocery, pharmacy, banks, and churches, are all within easy walking distance. The Gainsborough features social and recreational activities that enhance daily living for today's active senior and is run by the Salvation Army.

Our house sold within one week for a price higher than we had asked. Thanks again to our wonderful Shepherd! We began to see how our Scripture verse was unfolding right before our eyes. We were sad to leave our sweet home and good neighbours after ten happy years, but we also felt excited as God was definitely moving us towards the freedom of condo living. Within five weeks, on April 30th, 2003, we moved to 210-511 Gainsborough Road. We were fortunate to have many friends and Brian to help us that day.

One week after moving we discovered the Medway Valley Heritage Forest, just a five minute walk from our condo. A narrow path runs through the bush (wilderness) leading to Medway Creek where the water (streams) runs over the rocks, especially in the early spring. Have you just read words similar to these? It was absolutely amazing and exciting to see with our eyes and hear with our ears the complete fulfillment of Isaiah 43:18,19. The "path through the wilderness," and the "streams of water." Indeed, our Heavenly Father had so lovingly provided for us in an unmistakable way.

Further benefits of living in the Gainsborough included a two minute drive to Brian and Christine's home, and a ten-minute walk to Vera and Bill Tyler's home, where they lived with their daughter Maybeth, until their deaths. Remember Maybeth was the little girl I shared a bedroom with upon arriving in Canada 53 years earlier. In addition, West Park Baptist Church had relocated to property on Gainsborough Road, exactly a two-minute drive from our home. A shopping mall was five minutes away. What more could we ask for?

Not a day went by that we didn't thank the Lord for His generous provision. The Gainsborough has many amenities: a mini spa pool, work shop, indoor parking with a do-it-yourself car wash, a library, pool table, Bible studies, chapel, and weekly planned activities. Walter and I had a passion for table tennis which we played three times a week. The competition, fun, and laughter were so exhilarating!

By the end of July 2007, six years after moving into the Gainsborough, Walter's lung condition worsened. In addition, sales were diminishing due to competition from the main cemeteries in town who, up to this time, had sold plots, but not monuments. Changes in government regulations also negatively affected businesses both large and small. It was time to terminate our business after 30 plus years of hard, dedicated work. Amazingly, without advertising, God sent people in the monument trade, as well as office people, to our shop, offering to buy machinery and office equipment. Maybe they knew Walter's health wasn't good. How quickly the shop was emptied of all stock and equipment. The final day found us sweeping up the remaining sand and leaving the shop for good. By the fall of 2008, Walter was very ill, causing me to become full-time care giver. God knew what He was doing when He led me into nursing.

I often wonder how I would ever have managed during those days, months, and years without the support of CCAC (community care), the loving care of our church family, the love and help shown by friends within the Gainsborough family, and, of course, our own family.

In September 2008, I began a "Kindness and Thank You" journal. What a precious little book this has become. It is a special joy to re-read and therefore remind myself of how our Shepherd used various people to bless us. Examples of kindnesses included: delicious meals brought to us, (one dear friend continually left fruit and juice outside the door for us to discover), monetary gifts arrived at just the right time, the use of a walker and a wheelchair, folks who sat with Walter to give me a break, visits with friends, and the list goes on. I experienced again that

"A true friend reaches for your hand and touches your heart."[2]

Derrick, the Personal Support Worker, acquired through the CCAC, faithful and cheerfully came to bathe and attend to Walter's personal needs. The two of them enjoyed talking of their love for football and of their relationship with God. Derrick won several well deserved awards for his professional work. It was easy to see why. It was most gratifying for him to become a part of our daily lives.

Early in December 2008, Brian and I drove to Toronto to visit my sister Marjory who was living in Nisbet Lodge, next door to Calvary Church. We went to help her prepare Christmas cards.

We were looking forward to experiencing Marjory's gracious company and delightful sense of humour. We were not disappointed.

Little did we know that within the next two days, on December 2nd, Marjory would be in Heaven! She had anticipated this wonderful day for so long. That final visit with her became so precious. It took me a few days to realize that I was now the only living member of my immediate family.

The next day her body was transported to Mount Pleasant Cemetery in London for burial. Cousin Don Perkins led a short service attended by several friends. My vivid memories of this day included a very cold wintery day and the kindness of Brian's co-workers who offered to be pallbearers. My Shepherd was again caring for me.

I had just one week to arrange for Marjory's Memorial Service at Calvary Church. Lorraine and Jim helped me with this. Gordon and Lynne Tyler graciously drove me to Toronto early in the morning. Brian and Christine arrived later and their support meant much to me. Brian Gibson from OMF spoke of Marjory's challenging experiences during her school days in China. Ladies from the church provided a nice luncheon. A thoughtful neighbour came to stay with Walter from 6 to 8 am. Then a nurse stayed with him for the rest of the day. I was so thankful for this, but thought how precious it would have been to have him with me that day.

I also realized how much I would miss my dear sister with whom I had finally created a strong bond during the last few years. It had never been my privilege to live with her in a normal home setting during my entire life!

Marjory led a full life in spite of much physical suffering and distress as a result of her days in the Weihsien concentration camp. Upon receiving her Bachelor of Religious Education degree at Gordon College in Boston, she worked with ISCF, taught school in Toronto, worked with World Vision, and the Africa Inland Mission. She was a meticulous proof reader, and editor. She possessed an excellent command of the English language. Those who knew her well agree that her gift for writing and her musical gift on the piano were displayed in a truly humble and Christ-like manner. Her battle with cancer brought a special tone to her more than 80 poems. Many people received encouragement by reading these. She will be remembered as a kind, gracious lady, whose sweet spirit showed absolutely no bitterness for the tragic circumstances of her life. A sample verse from one of Marjory's poems;

It is easy to be discouraged
When looking at your life,
Perhaps feeling that you have failed,
Or weary with daily strife.
But think about this fact -
And it is really true -
That the great God Almighty
Finds His pleasure in you!

I had been appointed as my sister's Executor. But how was I to deal with the increasing amount of file folders clamouring for my attention as well as increasing my care for Walter? The dining room table solved this dilemma by becoming my office. File folders contained Walter's medical papers, including meticulous daily journals of his condition, and Dancy Memorials business books. I still did the monthly business accounting because the business wasn't officially closed as yet.

As Executor for Marjory, I had to work with her lawyer in Toronto. That was a nightmare until we hired a new lawyer. Many Government documents were required. I continued doing our own personal finances. Again, I kept exacting budget book accounts and often worked into the early morning hours.

In the midst of all this, several times I had to take Walter to Emergency for urinary problems. Each visit was a challenge due to his shortness of breath. Eventually surgery was required, but we were warned that the anesthetic would be a risk for his lungs. We sent out an SOS for prayer support and the Lord brought him through this successfully. I will always remember the surgeon emerging from the OR door with both his thumbs pointing up and displaying a broad smile! We could breath easily at last! If only Walter could have done so, as well! It was comforting to have Lorraine and Christine with me that morning.

How grateful we were to have the privilege of celebrating our 50th Wedding Anniversary on March 5, 2010. Our children, grandchildren, a few family members and friends joined us in the Lawson room at the Gainsborough. This was our opportunity to thank each person present, for the specific way he or she had touched our lives.

Our children did a splendid job of helping me to plan this event. Sadly, Walter was not feeling very comfortable as his breathing was laboured but he was so sweet and tried his best to cope. I was so proud of him and yet inside, my heart ached for him. Two weeks later Walter's oxygen level was low enough to require nasal oxygen. This new experience quickly became a part of our lives as we adjusted to watching the oxygen levels to avoid a crisis and order new tanks when necessary. It was a relief for Walter to breathe more easily. This enabled us to go to the various doctors' appointments with the tank hooked onto the wheelchair.

In the spring of 2010, Walter's sister Gladys, was diagnosed with a fast growing brain tumour. What a shock for her immediate family especially, and also for us. Gladys often popped in to see Walter, bringing her usual goodies along with encouragement. With great effort on Walter's part, I took him to visit Gladys at home, his last time to see her. Often this special sister and brother duo talked on the phone together, even when Bill and I needed to support the phones for each of them. They kidded each other as to who was going to win the race to Heaven.

Gladys died on November 15, 2010. I could tell that Walter felt her death keenly. I did my best to calmly prepare us both for her Memorial Service, which we knew would be his last outing. The service was a real tribute to Gladys, and God was honoured in a wonderful way.

I had a difficult time shielding Walter from all the people who wanted to talk with us. With Brian and Lorraine's help we left the service quickly. Lorraine drove from Ottawa for the service. She loved Aunt Gladys very much and is like her in creative and musical traits.

By the beginning of May 2011, Walter required constant care, and I was wearing out. After consultation with the Nurse Practitioner, Brian, Christine, and Lorraine in Ottawa, we felt it was time to take him to University Hospital. I asked Walter if he would mind going there.

His answer: "Whatever is best for you, Dear!" That was so typical of him. That day was Mother's Day, May 8, 2011.

The morphine dosage at home wasn't enough to keep Walter free of pain. The increased dosage given in hospital relieved a lot of pain, relaxing him enough to display his humour as never before, giving family and staff some good laughs. This helped to relieve the increasing strain we felt, knowing this to be the beginning of the end.

Dr. Sharon Baker, head of the Palliative Unit, chose Walter along with three other patients, to participate in a documentary done by the CBC. It is called, "A Good Death." The patients shared their thoughts regarding their impending death. As Walter had just received morphine prior to the photographer coming into his room, he was able to speak clearly about his personal trust and faith in the Lord Jesus and how ready he was to be on his way to Heaven any day. He finished by saying, "You can't take anything from this life with you, except your faith in the Lord." Walter always smiled when Dr. Baker entered his room. She was a dear.

Because the photographer knew we had been married for 51 years, she took a photo of our hands together displaying our wedding rings. This picture was shown on the CBC Documentary, prior to the related interviews. People could view this online for several years. How precious it was for me to click on this site and see and hear Water speak briefly. Our granddaughter, Rachel, watched it over and over many times. She was so close to her Papa and missed him ever so much. Didn't we all!

Walter referred to his approaching death by saying, "When my flight takes off," or "I wish my flight would come soon." That wish came true and his flight to Heaven departed on May 31st, 2011 at nine in the evening. Lorraine, Brian, and Christine were with me. I cannot explain how I felt emotionally that hour. My dearly loved husband was gone—for the present. I know I will join him when my turn comes, for I share the same strong faith and trust in the Lord Jesus that Walter did.

Up until then, I thought *widowhood happened only to other wives, not me*. I asked the Lord to help me accept the fact that it was now my turn. Many years earlier, I had asked my mother why the Lord allowed the accident that killed my father, to happen, leaving her a widow at age 41. I remember her answer: "So that I would depend entirely on Him for my strength and future needs and have a closer relationship with my Heavenly Father." I knew that I had to find comfort and strength from the Scriptures each day, just as my mother had done. Somewhere in my readings I found this phrase: "Life may not be great — but you have Me. Signed, God."

Dr. Kevin Rutledge, then pastor of West Park Church, had been a kind and caring visitor at home and at the hospital. As he conducted the Memorial Service along with son-in-law, Jim, we all felt the presence of God throughout this most precious time of remembering Walter. How beautiful to see our four granddaughters on the platform as Sarah read each of their thoughts of Papa/Grampy. Walter had asked Lorraine to play a piano solo "It is Well with My Soul." She and Brian gave tribute to their dad by using a suitable word from each letter of the alphabet. A good friend, Dave Shadd, who had visited Walter many times at home and in the hospital, gave a loving tribute. Dave is with Walter in Heaven now.

Walter was greatly loved and respected by many people. He was known for his kindness and quiet humble manner. His main gift was to greet folk each Sunday morning at the church door. He made them feel welcome in a special way, always remembering their names and often connecting them to another person with a common link. He trained others in this special skill and people at West Park continue to speak about Walter Dancy and his special gift.

Chapter 12
God's Surprises

"Trust in the Lord with all your heart and
lean not on your own understanding;
in all your ways acknowledge him,
and he will make your paths straight."
Proverbs 3:5,6

Nearly three months following Walter's death, it was a pleasure to attend Lorraine and Jim's daughter Sarah, and Christopher Bastian's wedding in Ottawa. Such fun it was to travel there with Brian, Christine, Rachel and Michelle. When we arrived, however, I discovered I had forgotten my big suitcase. For someone who likes everything to be in order, this was a disaster. I had heard that a new widow may forget or do unheard of things, due to the stress of adjusting to a new normal. That was me, all right! A month before, I had mistakenly purchased incorrect train tickets when visiting out of town friends. What would be next, I wondered? Help!

I wept into my pillow that night because of the uncertain challenges that lay ahead. Lorraine was relieved when she found I had brought my outfit for the wedding in a separate little suitcase. Thankfully, I could fit into my daughter's clothes and spent the next week wearing them.

The wedding was perfect. It was held outside at the groom's home, in a country setting. Attending this special family event, as a grandmother of the bride, meant much to me even though not having Walter with me was so hard. I felt it keenly especially during family photo time. It must be noted here that Jason and Deb Ransom were none other than the photographers for Canada's former Prime Minister, Stephen Harper! Jim had married them and was their pastor in Ingersoll. Furthermore, both Sarah and Lorraine also had taught their children piano lessons. Indeed, it was a special privilege to meet them.

In the fall of 2011, several weeks after Sarah and Christopher's wedding, I began attending a 13-week seminar called "Grief Share" at West Park church. The timing was right for me: three months into widowhood. The two ladies leading this course were most understanding and sensitive to each of the attendees, having suffered losses of their own. We received helpful information and watched practical DVD's. Also a delicious dinner was served prior to the evening sessions. I began to feel stronger in my spirit, knowing that my dear Shepherd was taking care of me in spite of the waves of emotions that engulfed me from time to time.

The first year is most difficult as the bereaved person faces what is called "the first of facing an event since..." These dates or "ambushes" can be overwhelming unless we lean heavily on God for courage. His promises are right there in the Bible for us to grasp.

In addition, I strived to keep limber by continuing to play table tennis three times a week. An added benefit of this activity was the gales of laughter that accompanied it. Can you imagine my now four-foot-eleven inch frame climbing under the table to recover roaming ping pong balls, not once but many times!

Dancy Memorials was inactive for the years that Walter was ill, and I wanted to have the business officially closed before 2011 ended. As well, November had always been our Year End, so it made sense to follow suit. My lawyer and I worked, watched, and prayed as we dealt with the bank's lawyers. Would I have to clear the outstanding sum completely? I couldn't face that possibility. This was one of many times, if not the most crucial time, that my faith and trust were tested. God guided my pen as I wrote a Letter of Settlement which was well received by the bank's lawyers. God miraculously brought the business to closure before our Year End, with a mutual agreement by both parties. During the three months of closing, I had relied heavily on promises from the Scriptures:

"Present your case" says the Lord"
"Set forth your arguments" says Jacob's King
Isaiah 41:21
"For I am the Lord you God,who takes hold of your right hand
and says to you, Do not fear; I will help you"
Isaiah 41:13

During this time I was reading *The Red Sea Rules* by Robert J. Morgan which gives God's ten strategies for difficult times. These were just what I needed! It was exciting to see how God was bringing me through a critical experience. I called it "my own Red Sea crisis." It is when we are tested and find ourselves in the tightest corners of life, that we have to trust God implicitly. How fortunate I was to have a competent and understanding lawyer, who was a gem to work with, both in business and personal matters such as closing Walter's affairs. I also had mixed emotions as I left the accountant's office for the last time. Their staff had served Dancy Memorials well, keeping us in line for so many years. Two of our memorial associates each planted a tree in memory of Walter. Brian and I attended one Tree Planting Ceremony at a conservation park in Sarnia. The second tree was planted in Israel! This notification came with a beautiful card and appreciation for Walter. These meaningful gestures were heart warming for me and the family.

With the knowledge of my Shepherd's care of me throughout the past years, I knew He would continue to guide me in the years ahead. My children made sure I wasn't alone for the first Christmas and spending it in Ottawa with Brian and Lorraine and their families was so comforting.

I took two train trips on my own that second summer. One was to Burlington where my cousins, Mary and Stirling lived. As well, I enjoyed lunch with three nursing school classmates. The other visit was to Peterborough staying with good friends, and renewing friendships made over 30 years before. They arranged lunch at a Tea House. It was such a happy occasion, visiting with three other nurses from days gone by. It was the first time that the four of us had been together. This was certainly a refreshing experience for me, and it gave me more confidence to face new situations.

During Walter's illness, on a treacherous winter day near Christmas, I had met a gentleman in the hallway. He was debating whether to go out into the storm to buy milk. I decided to give him a bag of milk. After all it was Christmas! After delivering the milk, I wished him a "Merry Christmas." After that he occasionally came to visit Walter just chatting about this and that.

Several months after Walter's death, this gentleman began to show some interest in me, even taking me out for dinner a few times. Imagine my surprise to find that he had been a shepherd in England and Scotland. A sheep farmer, no less! What a coincidence, with my passion and love for sheep! He kindly gave me several sheep mementoes from England which I will always treasure. In turn, I gave him a copy of my favourite book, *A Shepherd Looks at Psalm 23,* by Phillip Keller. Even with the gift of one dozen roses for my birthday, I didn't feel this relationship should be continued. I was grateful, however, for the time spent with the shepherd from The Gainsborough. My own Shepherd, my Heavenly Father, was preparing for me an unexpected blessing of His choosing. Keep reading, my friends!

Our brother-in-law, Bill, had often come to visit Walter and me following his wife's death. During one of those visits, the subject of remarriage popped up. I casually said, "I will never marry again, but I wouldn't mind going out for dinner with a Christian gentleman." Widows often say words similar to those for various reasons. My reason was I felt I'd never find someone like Walter ever again.

Fast forward to one-and-a half years later. Bill began asking me out for dinner every few months purely as a friend and brother-in-law. We both shared the loss of our spouses who had been brother and sister. Not until the tenth time when we went out for dinner on July 24, 2012, did the thought of romance begin to surface. Bill held my hand as we walked on the beach at Port Stanley just south of London. I told him that there was no one I would rather be with than him. I can not believe I said that! Apparently that statement was prompted by God. Those words were the very ones Bill needed to hear for the answer to his prayer for the right choice of a woman to be his wife. That week was my birthday – the same birthday when the shepherd from The Gainsborough gave me the roses. Bill treated me to a lovely dinner followed by a fantastic concert at the Grand Theatre. Yes, we both had fallen in love.

Although we had known each other for over 50 years, the next five months were busy as we began to find out more about each other, and our soon-to-be blended five children and ten grandchildren, including one in Heaven.

Bill's sister, Carol, many years ago married Gerry Brock, of the same Brock family I knew during the 1960's at Wortley Baptist Church. So there are many Brocks on both sides of our families.

Bill had retired from the London Board of Education as a school principal. It was exciting to travel with him to Ohio to meet his close friends, Wendell and Sue Brown, and to gain their approval. I passed the test! How I love them! That was in September 2012.

With the permission and blessing of our children, we were engaged two months later in November. What a blessing it was to have our families enthusiastically support us. Everyone at our wedding on December 28th, 2012 including the minister and musicians, were all family members. We used the facilities at The Gainsborough with their lovely chapel and dining room where we enjoyed a delicious catered meal. And so began a new married life. So much for my determination never to marry again! My loving Shepherd, again had provided for someone to love and care for me.

A week after the wedding, in January 2013, Bill and I flew to Boca Raton, Florida, for a week-long honeymoon. It was a delight to view the Atlantic ocean again after not seeing it since I was a teenager coming to Canada. The balmy weather was glorious. Bill was familiar with this area and had friends near by. He introduced me to a delightful family who had long ago accepted Bill as their "uncle." They were the children of the Browns whom I had met in September. Now I understood why they had been Bill's "family by choice" for over forty years.

Once back home, it was time to move my household goods from The Gainsborough to Bill's home, now my new home. No, OUR new home! It meant so much to have Lorraine come from Ottawa to ably assist me. I had the apartment repainted and put up for sale at the beginning of March. It was not easy to leave The Gainsborough and all it had meant to me. The move to a house after ten years in a much loved condo was a challenge. However, we gladly accepted these adjustments knowing that God had brought us together. My condo sold within the year for which we were very thankful. God used a much admired friend to spark the sale. It is exciting to watch how God works things for good, when we belong to Him.

My first of many holidays with Bill began when we spent the month of March in Fort Myers, Florida. His good friends, Dan and Phyllis McTavish are there each winter, and we have spent time with them in the same Mobile Home Park for the past four winters. They are special friends indeed, so gracious, kind, and "given to hospitality."

It has been my privilege to speak about my childhood days in China to various groups. Much of what I say, you have just finished reading. Bill joined me during these talks by being my interviewer which gave more insight and humour for the audience. Usually I wear a Chinese silk brocade jacket that was given to me, and I hold a 25" stuffed sheep! So both reflections of my life come into play. Yes, I still love my many sheep!

I now look back and see how God provided for me in each new circumstance: the unsettled life as a young missionary's child, the love, security and provision of three sets of guardians, nurses training, marriage to Walter, raising two dear children with the many moves we made, owning a business for 35 years, Walter's death, closing the business, selling the condo, and marrying Bill. In each of these experiences, (some were extremely tough) I had an opportunity to trust my Heavenly Father or go it alone. And each one was WRAPPED IN LOVE.

The years since I married Bill have been a blessing, full of adventure and new experiences. There is never a dull moment when Bill is around! Indeed, my faithful Shepherd has taken care of me as promised in Isaiah 46:4

"Even to your old age and gray hairs I am he,
I am he who will sustain you.
*I have made you and I **will carry** you;*
I will sustain you and I will rescue you." (emphasis mine)

I never dreamed this verse would have so much meaning for

me later in life. I had taken this verse to be mine as I faced the unknown future. Have you detected the **Will**iam **Carey** name in this verse? I did! Yes, one letter is askew, I must admit.

Our marriage meant a change of churches for me and now I have a new set of friends. Of course, I still "have a cuppa" with my long time friends from West Park Church and The Gainsborough. Our marriage has enabled us both to bond closer with our children and grandchildren, sharing in their joys and praying for them in their down times. I'm not just an aunt anymore to my nieces and nephew, Bill's children. I'm now a step-mother to them: Alicia (and Rob Phelps), with Courtney and Nicole, David (and Alison) with Noelle, and Grace (and Scott Bull) with Ryan and Matthew. It is a joy to be a part of this family and also to be a part of Bill's retirement years.

My expectation was that my story would finish with my marriage to Bill. However, an exciting event has happened since. Sarah and Christopher welcomed a baby boy in December 2015. His name is Caleb James, and we are so pleased. Bill teases me about the adjustment of him being married to a great-grandmother, but after all, I have to adjust to being married to a great-great uncle! Lorraine and Jim are mighty proud first time grandparents. Hannah, of course, is very happy to be an aunt.

Life goes on and I take refuge in continuing to trust my Good Shepherd, whatever the future holds. How blessed my life has been. I do hope that you, my dear readers, whether family member or friend, have been encouraged and blessed by reading the story of my life. Thank you

Brian and Christine

Lorraine and Jim

Marjory later in life

Bill and Helen's wedding – December 2012

Walter

Granddaughters - L to R: Hannah, Sarah with husband Chris, Rachel, and Michelle.

Sources

Preface

1. Selwyn Hughes, *Every Day With Jesus* copyright Crusade World Revival (CWR)
2. Selwyn Hughes, *Every Day With Jesus* copyright CWR
3. Mrs. Charles Cowman, *Springs in the Valley*, August 17. Cowman Publishers, Inc. 1939
4. Phillips Brooks (December 13, 1825 - January 23, 1893) was an American Episcopal clergyman and author, who is remembered for writing the Christmas hymn, "0 Little Town of Bethlehem."

Chapter 1: "Don't Cry, Mummy"

1. Bishop Houghton, *China's Millions*, November 1941

Chapter 2: Beginnings

1. Jared Brock, *Living Prayerfully* Tyndale House, Used with permission.
2. William G. Windsor, *China's Millions*, August 1926
3. William G. Windsor, *China's Millions*, March 1927

Chapter 4: Meanwhile – Marjory

1. Charles R. Swindoll, www.AZQuotes.com, September 5, 2016
2. Dr. David Michell, *A Boy's War,* *OMF Publishers, 1988, Used with permission.
3. Dr. David Michell, *A Boy's War,* OMF Publishers, 1988, Used

with permission.

4. Dr. David Michell, *A Boy's War*, OMF Publishers, 1988, Used with permission.

(*Overseas Missionary Fellowship)

Chapter 5: Slow Boat to China

1. Selwyn Hughes, *Everyday with Jesus,* copyright CWR
2. Dr. David Michell, *A Boy's War*, OMF Publishers, 1988, Used with permission.
3. Sheila Miller, *Pigtails Petticoats and the old School Tie*, OMF Publishers, 1981, Used with permission.

Chapter 6: Adventures of a Teenager

1. Mrs. Charles Cowman, *Springs in the Valley*, July 5, 1939, Cowman Publishers, Inc. 1939
2. Hunting Stewart Tartan. www.tartansauthoritv.com
3. Royal Stewart Tartan. https://en.wikipedia.org/wiki
4. www.ivcf.ca Cathie Nicoll

Chapter 8: Setting up a Home

1. Charles Swindoll, taken from *When You Don't See His Plan*, 2011 Nadine Hennessey and Rebecca Baker, Discovery House, Grand Rapids, MI, Used with permission.

Chapter 9: The Shepherd's Plans

1. Mrs. Charles Cowman, *Springs in the Valley*, September 18, 1939, Cowman Publishers, Inc.

Chapter 10: The Empty Nest

1. *365 Things You Should Know About Life* (November 2011) Barbour Publishers
2. *www.goodreads.com/quotes* -Abraham Lincoln
3. *Why God Made Granddaughters* - Copied from a wall plaque

4. *Riding the Wind*, Author Unknown

Chapter 11 - New Beginnings
1. Selwyn Hughes, *Every Day With Jesus* devotional, copyright CWR
2. www.saying.quotes: Heather Pryor/photoquoto.com

CPSIA information can be obtained
at www.ICGtesting.com
Printed in the USA
LVOW10s0513061216
515966LV00001B/2/P